D0462801

Nicotine and Tobacco

Drugs

Other books in the Compact Research series include:

Drugs

Heroin
Marijuana
Methamphetamine
Performance-Enhancing Drugs

Current Issues

Biomedical Ethics
The Death Penalty
Gun Control
Illegal Immigration
World Energy Crisis

COMPACT *Research*

Nicotine and Tobacco

by Clay Farris Naff

Drugs

ReferencePoint Press™

San Diego, CA

For more information, contact
ReferencePoint Press, Inc.
PO Box 27779
San Diego, CA 92198
www. ReferencePointPress.com

Picture credits:
AP/Wide World Photos, 13
Landov, 11
Suzanne Santillan, 34–37, 50–53, 66–68, 83–86

Series design:
Tamia Dowlatabadi

LIBRARY OF CONGRESS CATALOGING-IN-PUBLICATION DATA

Naff, Clay Farris.
  Nicotine and tobacco / by Clay Farris Naff.
    p. cm. — (Compact research series)
  Includes bibliographical references and index.
  ISBN-13: 978-1-60152-006-7 (hardback)
  ISBN-10: 1-60152-006-9 (hardback)
  1. Nicotine addiction. 2. Nicotine. 3. Smoking—Health aspects. 4.
Youth—Tobacco use. I. Title.
  HV5735.N32 2006
  613.85—dc22

                                                              2006033962

Contents

Foreword

66 **Where is the knowledge we have lost in information?** 99

—"The Rock," T.S. Eliot

As modern civilization continues to evolve, its ability to create, store, distribute, and access information expands exponentially. The explosion of information from all media continues to increase at a phenomenal rate. By 2020 some experts predict the worldwide information base will double every 73 days. While access to diverse sources of information and perspectives is paramount to any democratic society, information alone cannot help people gain knowledge and understanding. Information must be organized and presented clearly and succinctly in order to be understood. The challenge in the digital age becomes not the creation of information, but how best to sort, organize, enhance, and present information.

ReferencePoint Press developed the Compact Research series with this challenge of the information age in mind. More than any other subject area today, researching current events can yield vast, diverse, and unqualified information that can be intimidating and overwhelming for even the most advanced and motivated researcher. The Compact Research series offers a compact, relevant, intelligent, and conveniently organized collection of information covering a variety of current and controversial topics ranging from illegal immigration to marijuana.

The series focuses on three types of information: objective single-author narratives, opinion-based primary source quotations, and facts and statistics. The clearly written objective narratives provide context and reliable background information. Primary source quotes are carefully selected and cited, exposing the reader to differing points of view. And facts and statistics sections aid the reader in evaluating perspectives. Presenting these key types of information creates a richer, more balanced learning experience.

For better understanding and convenience, the series enhances information by organizing it into narrower topics and adding design features that make it easy for a reader to identify desired content. For example, in *Compact Research: Illegal Immigration*, a chapter covering the economic impact of illegal immigration has an objective narrative explaining the various ways the economy is impacted, a balanced section of numerous primary source quotes on the topic, followed by facts and full-color illustrations to encourage evaluation of contrasting perspectives.

The ancient Roman philosopher Lucius Annaeus Seneca wrote, "It is quality rather than quantity that matters." More than just a collection of content, the Compact Research series is simply committed to creating, finding, organizing, and presenting the most relevant and appropriate amount of information on a current topic in a user-friendly style that invites, intrigues, and fosters understanding.

Nicotine and Tobacco at a Glance

Prevalence

Nicotine, which occurs naturally in tobacco, is one of the most widely used drugs in the world. Globally, more than 1.1 billion people use tobacco.

History

Use of tobacco began among Native Americans at least 1,500 years ago. It spread to the rest of the world after Christopher Columbus's 1492 voyage to the New World.

Usage

Tobacco is smoked in various ways or chewed. By far the most common use of tobacco is in cigarettes.

Consumption Rate

Around the world, more than 15 billion cigarettes are smoked each day.

Geographic Trends

Smoking is declining in most Western nations, but it is on the rise in the developing world, especially Asia. One of every three cigarettes worldwide is smoked in China.

Addictive Effects

The nicotine in tobacco is highly addictive. Most people who start using tobacco find it difficult to quit, despite the health hazards tobacco use presents.

Carcinogenic Effects

Tobacco is responsible for 87 percent of lung-cancer deaths and for most cancers of the larynx, oral cavity and pharynx, esophagus, and bladder.

Other Health Effects

Tobacco damages virtually every organ in the body, including the skin. It contributes to heart disease and worsens diabetes.

Business

Tobacco companies make up a major international industry, with estimated annual revenues of $200 billion worldwide.

Laws

Nicotine is unregulated in the United States. The sale of tobacco to youths is illegal but commonplace.

Treatment

Nicotine addiction is generally treated by nicotine replacement therapy through gum or skin patches, which help the smoker break the tobacco habit.

Cessation Success Rates

Smokers who try to quit unaided have a failure rate of about 80 percent. Replacement nicotine and cessation programs cut the failure rate in about half.

Trends

In the United States, smoking rates have been falling since the 1960s. Today, about 22 percent of Americans smoke.

Overview

The Dangers of Nicotine

Nicotine is a highly addictive drug that occurs naturally in the leaves of tobacco plants. While nicotine can be a potent poison on its own, tiny quantities found in cigarettes causes harm by addicting the smoker to the other, even more harmful ingredients in tobacco. For example, the tar in tobacco is especially cancer causing. Thus, nicotine addiction leads to the deaths of some 435,000 American tobacco users each year, making it by far the leading cause of drug-related premature death. The dangers of alcohol and illegal intoxicants pale in comparison. Alcohol abuse causes the deaths of approximately 85,000 Americans annually, and all other addictive drugs trail far behind. Cocaine and heroin, for example, are responsible for only about 16,000 deaths a year.

Tobacco leads other causes of early death as well. Driving accidents, for example, claim just one-tenth the number of lives that tobacco does. The only hazard that comes anywhere near the deadliness of tobacco is obesity. Obesity raises the risk of cancer, diabetes, and coronary disease, all of which contribute to, at most, some 365,000 deaths annually in the United States.

The toll exacted by nicotine addiction is higher. Nicotine makes tobacco the leading cause of preventable death. This status is unlikely to

This tobacco farm in Kentucky has more than 2,000 acres of tobacco fields. Nicotine, which occurs naturally in tobacco, is one of the most widely used drugs in the world.

change in the near future, despite a rapid rise in the obesity rate and a significant drop in the rate of tobacco use in the United States. The prevalence of smoking among American adults remains above 20 percent, and the decline in U.S. tobacco use has been more than offset by a rise in global consumption.

A Global Health Threat

Worldwide, health officials forecast that tobacco use will lead to a cancer toll that exceeds any single cause of premature death in history. "We are looking at about 1 billion [cancer] deaths this century if present trends continue," says Judith Mackay, lead author of *The Tobacco Atlas*.[1] If accurate, that would indeed be a colossal toll, amounting to one-sixth of the present world population. To set this in perspective, consider that since 1981 AIDS, the worst contemporary epidemic, has claimed about 25 million lives, less than 3 percent of the projected tobacco toll. Put another way, 1 billion tobacco deaths is 5 times greater than the estimated 200 million people who died in all the wars and atrocities of the twentieth century.

There is general agreement that the reason people continue to use tobacco even after they become aware of the hazards and want to stop is nicotine. All tobacco contains nicotine. When a person smokes or chews tobacco, tiny quantities of the drug are carried into the bloodstream via the particles of tar that also occur in tobacco.

The amount of nicotine in a cigarette, typically 3 to 9 milligrams, is tiny. A milligram is a thousandth of a gram, which itself is only about the weight of a standard paper clip. Fortunately for smokers, not all of the nicotine in a cigarette makes it into the lungs. Some is destroyed by the heat of the burning cigarette.

If nicotine were present in tobacco in greater quantities, it would kill off tobacco users almost instantly. Nicotine is an extremely hazardous drug. It acts rapidly on the nervous system. It causes sudden jumps in blood pressure, heart palpitations, and at higher doses paralysis. A lethal dose may be as little as 40 milligrams. In fact, nicotine has long been a key ingredient in insecticide.

> **If nicotine were present in tobacco in greater quantities, it would kill off tobacco users almost instantly.**

For tobacco users, however, the most insidious feature of nicotine is its addictiveness. Most health experts do not consider the tiny quantity of nicotine in tobacco products a major health threat by itself. To be sure, long-term use of nicotine does have negative consequences. It contributes to wrinkling skin and hardening blood vessels. It destroys valuable proteins in the circulatory system.

Still, whatever harm nicotine causes directly is dwarfed by the cancer-causing properties of other tobacco ingredients. Scientists have identified more than 40 carcinogens in tobacco. Combustion worsens the situation;

Peter Jennings, longtime ABC News anchor and smoker, died on August 7, 2005, after a short battle with lung cancer. Some researchers claim to have identified more than 60 cancer-causing agents in cigarette smoke.

some researchers claim to have identified more than 60 cancer-causing agents in cigarette smoke. Most of these threats have complex chemical names, but they include solvents such as benzene and heavy metals such as cadmium. The role nicotine plays is to make it excruciatingly difficult to stop exposing oneself to this symphony of carcinogens.

Unlike many other addictive drugs, nicotine is not a narcotic. Since it does not impair cognitive functions, it can be used by people while carrying out normal activities. This makes steady tobacco consumption legally and socially acceptable in many cultures. Some people smoke almost constantly; even moderate smokers typically go through one pack a day. No other recreational drug can be used with such frequency. This frequent exposure amplifies the risks and makes quitting all the more difficult.

A Tough Habit to Break

The grip of nicotine addiction is extraordinarily powerful. Experts say that for some people withdrawal symptoms rival those of heroin and cocaine. Among the common nicotine withdrawal symptoms are craving, irritability, headaches, lack of concentration, sleeplessness, and increased appetite. These symptoms may begin within a few hours after the last cigarette, quickly driving people back to tobacco use. For some people, the craving continues for months.

Social environment and daily habit make a big difference, researchers say. For most tobacco users cigarettes or other tobacco products become part of their daily routine. Smoking, especially, becomes strongly associated in the mind of the smoker with various other habits such as drinking coffee, tea, or alcohol or with mealtimes. Additionally, a familiar setting such as a bar or restaurant where the individual has been in the habit of smoking and where others smoke can make it very difficult to resist falling back into the practice. A person who works in a setting where smoking is commonplace will typically find it much more difficult to quit than someone who works in a nonsmoking workplace.

Even personal relationships play a role. The old saying that "misery loves company" often comes into play; when someone attempts to quit, his or her friends who are smokers may tease or cajole the person into rejoining the fold of tobacco users. Conversely, a person who is encouraged to quit by others who are either also quitting or who are nonsmokers may find it easier to break the addiction. Whatever the circumstances, most people find quitting very difficult. The failure rate is extraordinarily high. According to the National Institute on Drug Abuse, smokers who attempt to cease the habit frequently relapse: Up to 80 percent of those who quit return to the habit within six months.

The Entrenched Status of Tobacco

You may wonder why a drug that nearly everyone, including the major tobacco companies, agrees is addictive and dangerous remains legal. The answer lies in history. When Christopher Columbus first arrived in the New World in 1492, Native Americans presented him with a gift of tobacco. Various tribes had been smoking the leafy plant for thousands of years, and some considered the practice an important part of sacred rituals. Columbus, however, thought so little of tobacco that he reportedly threw the gift overboard along with the ship's trash. All the same, as other Europeans voyaged to the Americas they began to bring tobacco back in increasing quantities. Noblemen in various European courts took up the habit of inhaling finely chopped tobacco leaves into their nostrils, a practice that came to be known as dipping snuff.

> " You may wonder why a drug that . . . everyone . . . agrees is addictive and dangerous remains legal. "

Tobacco gained a huge boost in prestige in 1560, when an amateur French naturalist, Jean Nicot, returned from Portugal with tales of the plant's miraculous medicinal properties—few of which turned out to be true. Nevertheless, Nicot, for whom nicotine is named, persuaded one of the most powerful monarchs of the time, Catherine de Médici, the queen of France, to give it a try. The queen had long suffered from migraine headaches. Nicot applied chopped tobacco leaves to her nose and forehead, and to her amazement, she found relief.

Ironically, research now shows that nicotine is a trigger for migraines; however, migraines are still poorly understood, and it is plausible that as a first-time user the queen experienced positive effects from nicotine. In any event, Catherine de Médici was so favorably impressed that she decreed that tobacco was henceforth to be called *Herba Regina*, the "Queen's Herb." To this day, tobacco enjoys particular prestige and popularity in France.

Yet nicotine did not remain in anyway the exclusive custom of the French aristocracy. Tobacco use spread from North America throughout Europe and Great Britain and later to the rest of the world. As colonists gradually occupied North America, tobacco cultivation became a major industry, especially in the South. Although some commentators at the time noted the association of smoking and lung disease, systematic knowledge of the hazards of tobacco was lacking, and claims about its healthful benefits persisted. Much romance surrounded tobacco. Mark Twain, arguably the most famous American of the 19th century, celebrated smoking in his novels and his speeches. As far as Twain was concerned, the more, the better. On the occasion of his 70th birthday, he remarked, "It has always been my rule never to smoke when asleep and never to refrain when awake."[2]

The Resistance to Scientific Findings

By the time medical science caught up with popular myths about tobacco, smoking was a well-established and widespread social custom. More importantly, it was a major U.S. industry with considerable influence among lawmakers.

Indeed, it was not until 1953 that scientists first demonstrated the carcinogenic properties of tobacco. Researchers who painted the backs of lab mice with tar from tobacco found that those mice developed cancerous tumors in far greater numbers than mice not exposed to tar.

> By the time medical science caught up with popular myths about tobacco, smoking was a well established and widespread social custom.

The tobacco industry responded to these and other experiments by trying to keep the public in doubt about the dangers of smoking and by trying to keep restrictions on tobacco and its contents to a minimum. Over the next several decades, consumer groups and health organizations battled to curb the sale of tobacco and to make its hazards known. The American Lung Association, which had formed decades earlier to fight the spread of tuberculosis, in 1960 declared that smoking was a major cause of lung cancer.

The tobacco companies, however, fought back hard and spent billions to suppress or discredit scientific research that questioned the safety of cigarettes, to limit regulation, and to stave off lawsuits. They largely succeeded. Although warnings on cigarette packages were mandated and tobacco advertising was limited, attempts to regulate nicotine as a drug were defeated. Congress passed a special exemption for nicotine, and the

Supreme Court later ruled that the U.S. Food and Drug Administration had to abide by Congress's decision.

By the mid-1990s, however, tobacco companies began to lose credibility. In hearings before Congress, tobacco company executives were compelled to admit that their product was addictive and dangerous. In a 1998 settlement with state attorneys general, tobacco companies agreed to stop advertising to youth and to give billions to antismoking campaigns.

In 2006 U.S. District Court Judge Gladys Kessler ruled that tobacco companies had intentionally deceived the public: "Cigarette smoking causes disease, suffering, and death. Despite internal recognition of this fact, defendants have publicly denied, distorted, and minimized the hazards of smoking for decades."[3] Tobacco companies were generally relieved that Judge Kessler did not subject them to monetary penalties, but at least one, Altria, and its subsidiary Philip Morris disputed her findings. "Philip Morris USA and Altria Group Inc. believe much of today's decision and order are not supported by the law,"[4] said William Ohlemeyer, an Altria vice president. The company intended to appeal, Ohlemeyer indicated.

Usage Trends

In the meantime, nicotine remains unregulated and tobacco remains a widely available legal product in the United States. Nevertheless, its popularity has been on the decline for several decades. U.S. cigarette consumption has fallen from its high in 1963, when about half of all men and one third of all women smoked, to the present, in which about one-fifth of the population smokes.

Despite the overall decline in American tobacco usage, until quite recently one group in the population remained enthusiastic about the product: teenagers. From 1991 through 1997, while tobacco use among the general U.S. population fell, the rate of youth smoking rose. Indeed, during that period about 3,000 youths under 18 became regular cigarette smokers each day, until well over a third of high school students were smokers. Following the cessation of marketing to youth with the 1998 master settlement between tobacco companies and the states, however, youth tobacco use has dropped steeply.

Smoking among high school students fell from about 35 percent in 1997 to 22 percent in 2003. Most researchers attribute this decline

> Nicotine remains unregulated and tobacco remains a widely available legal product in the United States.

to several factors: the end of such advertising as the "Joe Camel" campaign that targeted youth, the use of tobacco-settlement funds to pay for antismoking public education campaigns directed at young people, and the tightening of local laws against selling tobacco products to underage consumers.

The main reason for the overall decline in smoking is a growing awareness of the dangers of tobacco. Attempts to create a "safe cigarette" have so far failed. Low-tar, low-nicotine cigarettes have the paradoxical effect of making smokers smoke more as they struggle to satisfy their craving for nicotine. Late in 2005 British American Tobacco said it had developed a cigarette that would cut the disease risks by 90 percent, but health experts remained deeply skeptical. Nottingham University professor of epidemiology John Britton remarks, "Anything involving inhaling smoke is unsafe. These new cigarettes could be more like jumping from the 15th floor instead of the 20th—theoretically the risk is less but you still die."[5]

Such perceptions, along with the growing social stigma attached to smoking, have had a profound effect on tobacco usage rates in the United States. Additionally, external pressures on smokers to rein in or give up their habit have greatly increased. In particular, evidence of the hazard presented by secondhand smoke to nonsmokers has led to restrictions on smoking in the workplace, in public places such as schools and government offices, and in regulated places where people congregate, such as restaurants, theaters, and museums. Additionally, new taxes on cigarettes have raised the cost of smoking, and many insurance companies and employers offer incentives to smokers to quit.

These developments have not gone unchallenged. Smokers' rights groups have formed to fight bans on smoking in public places. Some deny outright the validity of the science that justifies restrictions on smoking. Others argue that libertarian considerations should outweigh the concerns of the government in regulating adult behavior. Despite their objections, however, across the United States restrictions on smoking have increased and the popularity of tobacco usage has fallen. Among the places a person can no longer legally smoke are prisons, hospitals, and airports. Beyond U.S. borders, however, a very different picture has taken shape.

The Global Rise

While Americans have curtailed their use of tobacco, worldwide consumption has been on the rise. Indeed, from 1970 to 1990 global cigarette sales leaped by 74 percent. One reason is increased prosperity in much of the world, especially Asia. Cigarettes, which used to be a luxury in countries such as China and India, are now widely affordable in the region. Thus, in 2004, Asia accounted for 56 percent of global cigarette sales.

An ironic contributor to the rise in tobacco consumption is the liberation of women. Smoking used to be an exclusively male privilege in most cultures. That has begun to change nearly everywhere, starting with the United States. Following the introduction of cigarettes marketed exclusively to women in the early 1970s, the rate of women's tobacco use in the United States rose sharply and is now closer to parity with men than anywhere else in the world. An unhappy consequence is that for American women born after 1960, early death from lung cancer is now on par with that of American men.

The same may soon be true around the world, where one of every five smokers is a woman. The World Health Organization has taken note of the trend: "Though fewer women than men are smokers, an increasing number of young women are taking up cigarettes. Recent reports describe an alarming increase in smoking rates among women. Further, data from different sources show the gap in smoking rates between men and women is narrowing."[6]

Women who take up tobacco use may find it extremely difficult to put down. Studies show that the addictiveness of nicotine affects women more powerfully than it does men. All other things being equal, these studies show, once hooked it is more difficult for a woman to quit than a man. That may be one reason why the rate of smoking has fallen much faster for American men than for women: Whereas U.S. male smoking prevalence dropped by 24 percent between 1965 and 1993, the prevalence of female smoking dropped by less than half that rate (only 11 percent) during the same period, according to the Centers for Disease Control and Prevention.

The global increase in smoking by both genders has led to an unprecedented health threat. Out of a world population of just over 6 billion, nearly 1 billion men and about 250 million women use tobacco. "More people smoke today than at any other time in human history. One person dies every ten seconds due to smoking-related diseases,"[7] notes Gro Harlem Brundtland, director general of the World Health Organization.

Tobacco is currently responsible for an estimated 12 percent of human mortality. With females rapidly joining the ranks of the world's smokers, health experts fear that the tobacco death toll will be much higher in generations to come. About one-third of the world's adult population is now addicted to a drug that exposes them to a high risk of fatal cancer and other ailments. "If current smoking patterns persist, there will be about 1 billion deaths from tobacco during the 21st century,"[8] note public health experts Richard Peto and Alan D. Lopez.

Hope for the Future

There are, however, some hopeful developments. Despite the addictive qualities of nicotine, many people successfully quit. One reason for this success is the rise of support programs to assist those who are quitting. These range from the annual World Smokefree Day (May 31) to commercial smoking-cessation programs in nearly every locality in America. Whereas in former times those who were ready to quit would usually trying going "cold turkey" (an apt description for the skin of a person in withdrawal), there are now sophisticated step-by-step programs that help a tobacco addict gradually taper off use of the substance until a fairly gentle permanent end can be attained.

Even more important has been the development of nicotine-replacement therapies. These typically involve nicotine-laced chewing gum or dermal patches. They give the addict a sufficient supply of the drug to stave off withdrawal symptoms while he or she works on behavioral changes to break the habits associated with using tobacco.

There is even some emerging evidence that nicotine—though not the

> There is even some emerging evidence that nicotine—though not the nicotine in tobacco—may prove to have medicinal applications.

nicotine in tobacco—may prove to have medicinal applications. Colleen McBride, director of the cancer prevention, detection, and control program at Duke University Medical Center, has experimented with treating various ailments with nicotine delivered through the same patches that are used to help smokers quit. McBride says that nicotine in controlled doses can be helpful. The benefits of nicotine, she claims, can be compared with those of caffeine. "Nicotine has a lot of therapeutic uses. There's growing evidence that it may be useful in treating Parkinson's disease, Alzheimer's—their level of concentration, their ability to focus. Those of us who are caffeine users understand that."[9]

Jean Nicot, who did so much to promote the belief that tobacco was healthful, would no doubt be gratified to know that the drug that bears his name may have some redeeming qualities after all.

All the same, for the vast majority of those who are regularly exposed to nicotine, it represents a mortal threat. It binds them to the tobacco habit, and that means an elevated risk of premature death from cancer, emphysema, heart disease, and other tobacco-linked pathologies.

So far, only the United States and a few other developed countries such as Britain have achieved significant reductions in tobacco use; yet, there are signs that others will follow. The Himalayan kingdom of Bhutan recently became the first country to entirely ban the sale of tobacco products. Iran has banned smoking in public buildings. Other countries are debating new restrictions on the use of tobacco as well. Many have signed an international tobacco-control convention, which, if enforced, could help curb smoking.

To be sure, not everyone believes that the global smoking rate will go down. Indeed, David Betteridge, a spokesman for British American Tobacco, the world's second-largest tobacco company, expects the market to grow. "Fewer people are smoking in percentage terms," he said in September 2006, "but because of huge population growth around the world, we are looking at a market about the same size in ten years' time, and beyond that maybe even bigger."[10]

However, if the United States, which has made large reductions in tobacco use, decides to join the international effort, the outcome might be different. An effective global treaty, health experts say, could pave the way to a world in which fewer people are at risk of premature and preventable death due to nicotine-driven addiction to tobacco.

How Harmful Are Nicotine and Tobacco?

> **Twenty percent of our nation's annual deaths are the result of side effects of nicotine dependence caused by cigarette smoking and other forms of tobacco use.**
>
> —Jack E. Henningfield, "Pharmacology of Nicotine," *Addicted to Nicotine: A National Research Forum.* May 19, 2006. National Institute on Drug Abuse. www.nida.nih.gov.

Nicotine is a toxic, psychoactive compound that occurs naturally in tobacco. Chemically, it is an alkaloid, or nitrogen-containing, substance. Pharmacologically, it is a fast-acting stimulant. Psychologically, it is a relaxant. Above all, however, nicotine is an addictive drug.

When smoked or ingested in minute quantities, nicotine rapidly enters the bloodstream and then acts within seconds on the brain. Its short-term effects vary. For most people, nicotine serves as a relaxant. In others, it acts as a mild stimulant. For virtually every user, though, the most notable fact about nicotine is its addictiveness. If it were not for the nicotine in tobacco, those who try to quit smoking would be spared cold sweats, sleeplessness, irritability, anxiety, appetite disruption, and intense craving. These are just some of the characteristics of withdrawal.

First-time users of nicotine feel its effects almost immediately as their heart pounds and skin tingles. These sensations are the result of nicotine's effects on the nervous system. It triggers a release of adrenaline, a hormone normally associated with the fight-or-flight reaction to a threat. Some people find the response exciting, but for many the effect soon turns to nausea and dizziness.

With continued tobacco use, the sensations change. The body becomes accustomed to the adrenaline jolt, and in many smokers it diminishes to the point where it is no longer noticeable. The effects of nicotine on the brain become more noticeable, however. Though not intoxicating, the drug has an effect similar to opiates such as heroin. Specifically, nicotine promotes the release of dopamine, a pleasure-inducing brain chemical. This relaxation response comes on rapidly but is fairly short-lived. Within a few hours at most, it is gone.

The Need for Nicotine Grows

The brain soon develops a tolerance for nicotine, which means that more is required to achieve the same satisfaction. Addiction quickly sets in. Once it does, symptoms of withdrawal occur if the nicotine supply is not frequently renewed. The time it takes to become addicted varies considerably. For some people it is a matter of a few days; for others, it is a few months. A small portion of users are able to dabble in tobacco without ever becoming addicted. This variation in response leads scientists to believe that there is a genetic predisposition to nicotine addiction that is stronger in some people and weaker in others.

The trouble with addiction to nicotine is how it is satisfied. More than 96 percent of nicotine addicts get their fix from cigarettes. Even those who use tobacco in other forms, such as cigars, pipes, or chew, are at risk, but cigarettes deliver tobacco smoke deep into the lungs, where it can do the most damage. Nearly all smokers start when they are teens, a time of life when caution is paid little heed. Moreover, the damage done by tobacco is slow and cumulative, so the risks are not apparent (even if they are known) at the time when addiction most commonly takes hold.

> " The onset of addiction can be especially swift for young people. "

The onset of addiction can be especially swift for young people. Researchers at the University of Massachusetts found that 12- to 13-year olds who smoked only a few cigarettes experienced the same symptoms of nicotine addiction as heavy-smoking adults. The researchers investigated 681 youngsters at schools in central Massachusetts over a four-year period. Some of the 12- and 13-year-olds became addicted within days of their first cigarette, according to research reported in 2000 in the British

Medical Association journal *Tobacco Control*. Prolonged use, even at a low level, had profound effects. Smoking only a few cigarettes a week caused kids to become as strongly addicted as adults who had been smoking for years. Richard Hurt, director of the Nicotine Dependency Unit at the Mayo Clinic, comments, "There's been a suspicion that many people become addicted very quickly, but this is really the first hard evidence that we've had that this occurs."[11]

How does a person know if he or she is addicted as opposed to just habituated? Researchers say that the length of time before a person has their first cigarette of the day after waking up is a pretty reliable indicator. Someone who typically feels the need to smoke within a half hour of getting out of bed is likely to be truly addicted.

A Tough Habit to Kick

Once addiction gets a grip, it can be extremely difficult to break the habit. An old smoking joke, attributed to Mark Twain, goes, "I can quit anytime I want. In fact, I've done it dozens of times already." In recent years, scientists have discovered that behind that joke is a stark truth: Nicotine is not only addictive, it is one of the most addictive substances known. In the brain, nicotine mimics the role of a natural neurotransmitter. That is, it docks at certain receptors in the brain that normally bind the neurotransmitter acetylcholine. As it happens, few brain chemicals are more important than acetylcholine. It plays a key role in relaying signals from neurons to muscles, focusing attention, and regulating memory. When nicotine enters the brain, it ramps up the effects of acetylcholine. Regular exposure to nicotine causes the brain to adjust to its presence. Some of the brain's acetylcholine receptors shut down. In other parts, transmission of chemicals speeds up or slows down in response to nicotine's effects.

When deprived of nicotine, an addict feels restless, inattentive, and has trouble concentrating, largely because the brain no longer functions normally without a supply of the drug. Moreover, nicotine promotes the release of dopamine in the brain. Dopamine activates the reward centers of the brain, giving rise to a pleasant, relaxed sensation.

Unfortunately, the body tends to become desensitized to the pleasurable effects of nicotine, meaning that it requires more of the drug to achieve satisfaction. Worse, once addiction sets in, a nearly constant supply of the drug is required to stave off unpleasant symptoms. Some studies suggest that it is easier to overcome an addiction to heroin than to nicotine.

When deprived of nicotine, an addict's nervous system flips into stress mode, with many painful and annoying consequences. Sweating, chills, and trembling are some of the common symptoms. Insomnia often follows. Most agonizing for the addict, however, is the constant craving felt within the brain. It is hard to fight yourself. As a consequence, the failure rate among would-be quitters is astronomical. One study shows that 80 percent relapse within 6 months. Longer-range studies show that, at least among those who attempt to go it alone, the failure rate is greater than 90 percent.

> **Some studies suggest that it is easier to overcome an addiction to heroin than to nicotine.**

The Challenges of Quitting

Once a person decides to quit, the first step is to reduce the amount of nicotine in the body. This takes time. The body's nicotine reserves drop by about half every 2 hours. At that rate, it can take up to 3 days for the blood to become nicotine-free. It is no coincidence that 3 days is how long a person who quits typically lasts before resuming smoking. Fortunately, there are now sophisticated cessation programs to help people gradually wean themselves from nicotine dependency. These programs help the brain resensitize itself and adjust to functioning normally in a nicotine-free environment. Moreover, the individual needs to develop new behavior patterns to break the conditioning that triggers tobacco use in dozens of situations. For example, many smokers are habituated to light up a cigarette when having a morning cup of coffee; such people may need to eat a carrot stick or switch to drinking cola in order to break the association of coffee and cigarettes.

The worst physical symptoms of nicotine withdrawal may persist for weeks. After that, the toughest challenges are psychological. The craving for nicotine continues, often infiltrating dreams or intruding into waking thoughts. In some people, this "knocking-on-the-door" phenomenon goes on for decades after they quit. Nevertheless, with motivation, determination, and support, it is possible to kick the habit. Millions of ex-smokers now lead healthier lives.

Since the federal government first approved the nicotine patch in 1992, nicotine-replacement therapy has greatly enhanced the success of cessation programs. Through the use of dermal patches or special chewing gum, addicts can obtain nicotine without tobacco. This allows them to begin making behavioral changes before they experience the withdrawal symptoms that accompany nicotine deprivation. Eventually they can taper off the use of nicotine replacement until they are entirely free of the drug. Although it remains painful to go through withdrawal, the science of tobacco provides all the motivation that many people need.

Chemical Assault

If nicotine is the engine of tobacco addiction, it pulls a long train of chemicals into the user's body. Tobacco is a complex plant, and cigarette manufacturers add hundreds of substances to it during the manufacturing process. Some are flavors, such as bay leaf and cinnamon, while others are better known as disinfectants, such as ammonia. In all, a cigarette may have as many as 599 additives. Once a cigarette is lit, combustion causes the chemicals to combine and recombine in a swirl of molecular activity. The smoke from cigarettes is astonishingly complex. It contains more than 4,000 chemicals. Of these, at least 43 and perhaps as many as 65 are carcinogenic.

> Since the federal government first approved the nicotine patch in 1992, nicotine-replacement therapy has greatly enhanced the success of cessation programs.

The health effects of these chemicals are equally varied, though nearly all are harmful. At one end of the spectrum of consequences is premature wrinkling. Smokers in their forties often have wrinkles similar to nonsmokers a decade or more older. Scientists say this is the result of tobacco smoke constricting the tiny blood vessels that nourish the underlying cells of the skin. (For similar reasons, smoking heightens the risk of impotence in men.) Less blood results in a thinner layer of skin, which is more easily wrinkled. A study of twins in which one smoked and the other did not found that the smoker had skin that was on average 25 percent thinner than the nonsmoker's.

Although wrinkles may be unattractive, other consequences of smoking are far worse. Certain chemicals in tobacco promote hardening and narrowing of the arteries. This, combined with the blood-pressure increase that nicotine induces, can lead to heart disease and stroke.

When a person smokes, tar and other chemicals blanket the lungs. Over time, the delicate air sacs known as alveoli struggle to stay alive. Shortness of breath results. If enough of the alveoli are damaged, emphysema results. This disease has been compared to drowning on land. People with emphysema often have to take oxygen tanks with them wherever they go just to get enough oxygen to remain alive.

The best-known consequence of smoking is lung cancer. The chemicals that pour into the lungs alter the DNA in the cells. Most often, such damage simply kills the cell. Eventually, however, cells may be damaged in such a way that they begin to reproduce wildly, forming tumors that spread throughout the body. Once this happens, even with aggressive treatment the survival rate is quite poor. Within two years 75 percent of those diagnosed with lung cancer die.

Although the vast majority of lung cancer cases occur in smokers—up to 90 percent by some estimates—not every smoker will develop lung cancer. In fact, the disease claims only about one in five regular smokers, with others succumbing to tobacco-related health effects and a fortunate minority remaining unscathed.

About 40 percent of smokers will live past the age of 65. Yet, for that lucky minority, another peril awaits. Seniors account for about 40 percent of those who die in cigarette fires, according to the National Fire Protection Association. The inescapable conclusion is that the diminished mental capacities that accompany old age make seniors who smoke far more likely to fall asleep while smoking in bed. This horrific death claims the lives of 300 to 350 seniors each year, a small number compared with lung cancer deaths but notable all the same.

Tobacco addiction is the single greatest cause of premature death in the modern world. In the United States it accounts for nearly half a million fatalities a year; worldwide the annual toll is 5 million and climbing. By the same token, however, it is also the most preventable form of premature death.

How Harmful Are Nicotine and Tobacco?

66 Almost single-handedly, smoking has transformed lung cancer from a virtually unknown disease at the turn of the twentieth century to the leading cause of cancer death at its conclusion. 99

—Kenneth E. Warner, quoted in Brian D. Smedley and S. Leonard Syme, eds., *Promoting Health: Intervention Strategies from Social and Behavioral Research*. Washington, DC: National Academy Press, 2000, pp. 417–18.

Warner is director of the University of Michigan's Tobacco Research Network.

66 Estimates of deaths from smoking are based mostly on speculative mathematical projections and should be treated with much more skepticism than is currently the case. 99

—Joe Jackson, "The Smoking Issue," 2004. www.forestonline.org.

Jackson has been a classical performer, punk rocker, and swing musician. He also writes nonfiction essays on smoking and other subjects.

* Editor's Note: While the definition of a primary source can be narrowly or broadly defined, for the purposes of Compact Research, a primary source consists of: 1) results of original research presented by an organization or researcher; 2) eyewitness accounts of events, personal experience, or work experience; 3) first-person editorials offering pundits' opinions; 4) government officials presenting political plans and/or policies; 5) representatives of organizations presenting testimony or policy.

66 **With tobacco there is terrible withdrawal; it is almost impossible for a lot of people. I did; I went cold turkey, . . . grass was not difficult, alcohol not difficult, but tobacco—oh my god!** 99

—Larry Hagman, quoted in "Dallas Interviews: Larry Hagman," 2003. www.ultimatedallas.com.

Hagman gained fame as the star of the television shows *I Dream of Jeannie* and *Dallas*, then put his celebrity into antismoking advocacy with the 1987 film *Larry Hagman—Stop Smoking for Life*, the proceeds of which benefited the American Cancer Society.

66 **Nicotine is an addictive drug. That's why people smoke.** 99

—David Kessler, quoted in *Online Newshour*, "Smoke Screening," August 23, 1996. www.pbs.org.

Kessler was the U.S. Food and Drug Administration commissioner during the Clinton administration. He led the failed effort to regulate nicotine as a drug.

66 **Smoking harms nearly every organ of the body, causing many diseases and compromising smokers' health in general. Nicotine, a component of tobacco, is the primary reason that tobacco is addictive.** 99

—Nora D. Volkow, quoted in *NIDA Research Report—Tobacco Addiction*, NIH publication no. 06-4342, rev. ed., 2006. www.nida.nih.gov.

Volkow is director of the National Institute on Drug Abuse. Volkow received her medical degree in 1981 from the National University of Mexico at Mexico City and performed her residency in psychiatry at New York University.

66 The cigarette should be conceived not as a product but as a package. The product is nicotine. . . . Think of the cigarette pack as a storage container for a day's supply of nicotine. . . . 99

—William L. Dunn Jr., "Motive and Incentive in Cigarette Smoking," Philip Morris memorandum, 1971. www.umich. edu.

Dunn was a leading scientist and vice president of the Philip Morris tobacco company.

66 Just like smoking cigarettes, chewing smokeless tobacco can eventually rip apart your body and kill you. It's that simple, really. There's no such thing as a 'safe' tobacco product. 99

—Steven Dowshen, "Smokeless Tobacco," *KidsHealth*, September 2004. www.kidshealth.org.

Dowshen is chief medical editor of the KidsHealth Web site. He serves as a pediatric endocrinologist at the Alfred I. DuPont Hospital for Children in Wilmington, Delaware.

66 Many of the world's oldest people have smoked. Jeanne Calment smoked and rode her bicycle until the age of 100 and died at age 122. 99

—Smokers United, "We Are Americans, Too," 2001. www.geocities.com.

Smokers United is a smoking advocacy Web site that promotes a libertarian view of tobacco use.

❝You can't smoke a cigarette in a safe way. Cigarettes are the only thing that, if you follow the manufacturers' instructions, are likely to kill you.❞

—John Wyke, quoted in Kevin Mansi, "Banning Cigarette Ads Can Save Lives, Claims Expert," *Daily Record*, December 6, 2000. http://no-smoking.org.

Wyke is director of the Beatson Institute for Cancer Research, in Glasgow, Scotland.

❝It's never too late to eliminate the effects of tobacco on your body for both heart disease and for lung cancer, and for other cancers as well. But the most important thing I can tell young people or anybody is don't start smoking.❞

—Jay Brooks, quoted in Miranda Hitti, "Peter Jennings Loses Battle with Lung Cancer," *WebMD Medical News*, August 8, 2005. www.webmd.com.

Brooks is chief of hematology and oncology at the Ochsner Clinic in Baton Rouge, Louisiana.

Facts and Illustrations

How Harmful Are Nicotine and Tobacco?

- Each year an estimated 435,000 U.S. deaths are attributed to tobacco use, making tobacco the primary cause of premature death.

- Nicotine is a potent poison. As little as 40 milligrams of pure nicotine can result in total paralysis followed by death.

- The nicotine inhaled in cigarettes acts directly on the nervous system and brain within about ten seconds.

- Addiction to nicotine typically sets in within weeks of regular exposure. Some people become addicted immediately.

- Breaking addiction to nicotine is extremely difficult for most people. Experts say the substance is as strongly addictive as opiates such as heroin.

- Some 87 percent of lung cancer cases—roughly nine out of ten—are related to smoking.

- An estimated 25 million Americans will die of smoking-related diseases in this century.

- The U.S. Centers for Disease Control and Prevention estimate that tobacco-caused illnesses and deaths cost the U.S. economy $157 billion a year in losses.

How Nicotine Affects the Brain

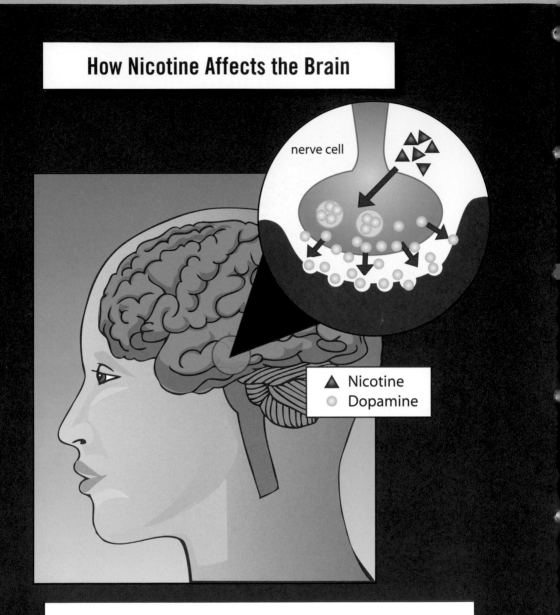

nerve cell

▲ Nicotine
● Dopamine

This illustration shows how nicotine affects the brain. After smoking or chewing tobacco, nicotine enters the bloodstream, stimulating the brain's production and release of dopamine. Dopamine is a chemical produced by parts of the brain that are involved in addictive behaviors. Although a user does not get a high from nicotine that one might get from drugs like cocaine and heroin, addiction to the drug can be powerful.

Source: NIDA Research and Report Series, 2005.

- Smokers' hands and feet often get cold because of damage to the circulatory system caused by tobacco.

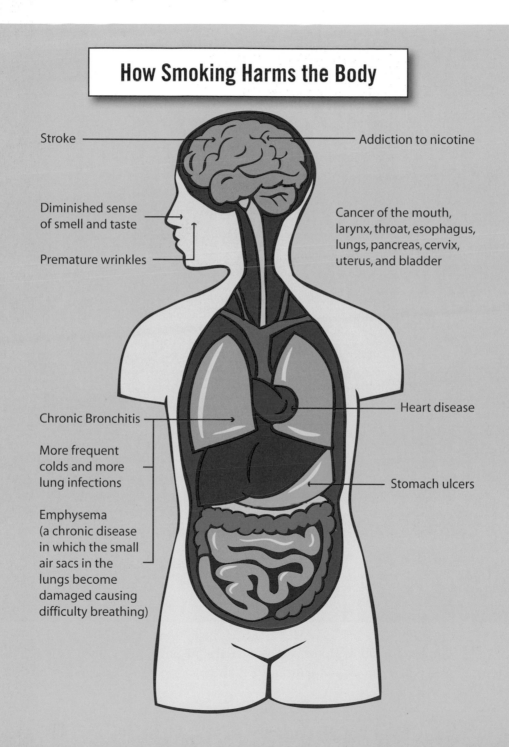

How Smoking Harms the Body

Stroke

Addiction to nicotine

Diminished sense of smell and taste

Cancer of the mouth, larynx, throat, esophagus, lungs, pancreas, cervix, uterus, and bladder

Premature wrinkles

Chronic Bronchitis

Heart disease

More frequent colds and more lung infections

Stomach ulcers

Emphysema (a chronic disease in which the small air sacs in the lungs become damaged causing difficulty breathing)

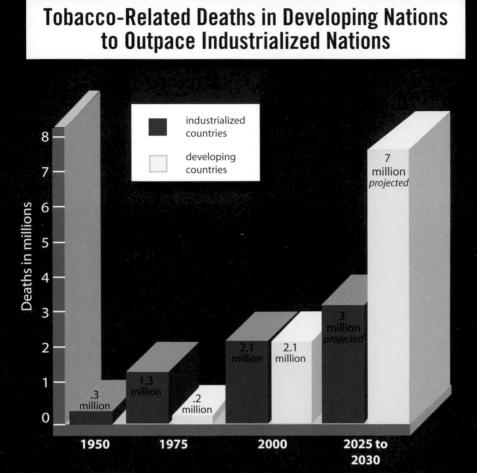

Tobacco-Related Deaths in Developing Nations to Outpace Industrialized Nations

This graph illustrates the growing impact of smoking and tobacco in developing countries, where annual deaths caused by tobacco are projected to more than triple by 2030. Tobacco-related deaths in industrialized countries, like the United States, will continue to increase but at a slower rate as long-running efforts to reduce smoking make a bigger impact.

Source: World Health Organization, *The Tobacco Atlas,* 2002.

- Long-term smokeless-tobacco users are 50 times more likely to develop oral cancer and gum disease, and to lose their teeth than non-users.

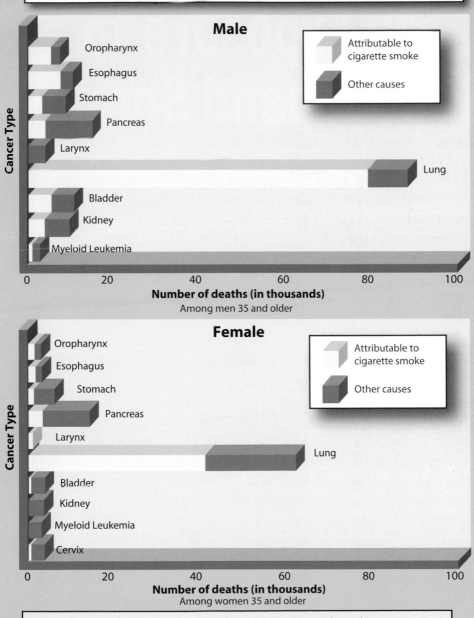

Average Annual Smoking-Related Cancer Deaths in the United States, 1995–1999

Male

Attributable to cigarette smoke

Other causes

Cancer Type

Oropharynx
Esophagus
Stomach
Pancreas
Larynx
Lung
Bladder
Kidney
Myeloid Leukemia

0   20   40   60   80   100

Number of deaths (in thousands)
Among men 35 and older

Female

Attributable to cigarette smoke

Other causes

Cancer Type

Oropharynx
Esophagus
Stomach
Pancreas
Larynx
Lung
Bladder
Kidney
Myeloid Leukemia
Cervix

0   20   40   60   80   100

Number of deaths (in thousands)
Among women 35 and older

These graphs illustrate the significant impact smoking has on cancer-related deaths. The majority of lung and esophageal cancer deaths are attributable to smoking, while pancreatic cancer seems to be more commonly influenced by causes other than smoking. Also, men are more likely to have a smoking-related cancer death than women are.

Source: American Cancer Society, Surveillance Research, 2005.

How Dangerous Is Exposure to Secondhand Smoke?

> 66 We . . . believe that the conclusions of public health officials concerning environmental tobacco smoke are sufficient to warrant measures that regulate smoking in public places. 99

—Tobacco company Philip Morris USA, 2006.

For nonsmokers, secondhand smoke used to be an annoyance, especially in restaurants, movie theaters, or other public places. Now, however, secondhand smoke is widely considered a serious health hazard. That recognition has not come easily, though, and it is still not universally accepted.

In 1992 the U.S. Environmental Protection Agency (EPA) released a report declaring environmental tobacco smoke (another term for secondhand smoke) to be a Class A carcinogen—that is, a substance that has been shown to cause cancer in humans. The EPA concluded that annually 3,000 Americans die of exposure to secondhand smoke. That figure has become widely disseminated but has also been hotly disputed.

In 1998 a federal judge found that the EPA had not followed proper procedures in coming to its conclusions. In his ruling U.S. District Court Judge William Osteen wrote, "In this case, EPA publicly committed to a conclusion before research had begun; excluded industry by violating the Act's procedural requirements; [and] adjusted established procedure and scientific norms to validate the Agency's public conclusion. . . ."[12]

However, that was not by any means the last word on the subject. As with all questions of science, ultimately the facts settle the issue. Since the 1990s, data have continued to accumulate. One of the facts that has been ascertained is that secondhand smoke contains the same chemical brew inhaled by smokers. The combustion of cigarette tobacco produces more than 4,000 chemicals in the smoke. More than forty are on the U.S. Department of Health and Human Service's report of known human carcinogens. Among them are benzene, formaldehyde, and nickel. Consequently, in 2000 the department formally listed secondhand smoke as a known human carcinogen in *The U.S. National Toxicology Program's 10th Report on Carcinogens.*

In the meantime, other agencies, public and private, have weighed in. The state of New York passed the Clean Indoor Air Act in 2003. According to the New York Department of Health, the measure was intended to eliminate nonsmokers' exposure to secondhand smoke. It did this by banning all smoking in public indoor locations, including restaurants and bars. The justification cited by the department was acute and chronic harm that results from exposure to secondhand smoke. In determining how great that harm might be, New York relied in part on developments on the West Coast.

> " California . . . has taken official action to classify secondhand smoke as a "toxic air contaminant." "

California, often a trendsetter for the rest of the nation, has taken official action to classify secondhand smoke as a "toxic air contaminant." The state's Environmental Protection Agency made its own estimate of the national mortality rate from secondhand smoke, projecting an even higher toll than the national EPA: 3,400 deaths a year from lung cancer and more than 60,000 fatalities a year from heart disease.

Antismoking advocacy groups cite these and other figures in arguing for restrictions on exposure to secondhand smoke. According to the American Lung Association, for example, "While smokers themselves face serious health risks from tobacco, it is now clear that even people who don't smoke may be threatened. Exposure to secondhand smoke may have certain harmful—possibly even fatal—health effects such as lung cancer and heart disease."[13]

Health officials say that cancer and coronary disease are not the only causes for concern when it comes to secondhand smoke. They also associate the following noncancerous conditions with exposure to environmental tobacco smoke: chronic cough, phlegm, wheezing, chest discomfort, reduced lung function, severe respiratory tract infections such as bronchitis and pneumonia, asthma, eye and nose irritation, and perhaps a worsening of cystic fibrosis for those who suffer from that disease.

Children at Risk

The exposure of children to secondhand smoke is especially harmful, tobacco researchers claim. Concerns begin with pregnancy. Although smoke itself does not reach the fetus, harmful ingredients in tobacco smoke do. Babies born following fetal exposure to secondhand smoke tend to have weaker lungs and are more susceptible to lung infection. During infancy, babies exposed to tobacco smoke suffer a higher rate of sudden infant death syndrome, according to the U.S. surgeon general.

Babies and young children are especially vulnerable to the effects of smoke because their lungs are still developing. According to the American Lung Association, secondhand smoke is responsible for up to 300,000 acute cases of pneumonia and bronchitis a year in children 18 months and younger. At least 7,500 of such cases are severe enough to result in hospitalizations.

> **Babies and young children are especially vulnerable to the effects of smoke because their lungs are still developing.**

According to the American Academy of Otolaryngology, exposure to secondhand smoke decreases lung efficiency and impairs lung function in children of all ages. It contributes to both the frequency and severity of childhood asthma. Secondhand smoke also aggravates a number of respiratory problems in children, such as sinusitis, rhinitis, cough, and postnasal drip. It also increases the number of children's colds and sore throats.

Critics Dispute the Dangers

Some critics, however, are unsatisfied that any of these findings have been established by rigorous science. The mere presence of carcinogens in smoke, they argue, does not mean that a person exposed to second-hand smoke will necessarily contract cancer or even be at significant risk. To determine that requires additional study and classification. To date, such critics say, studies have been sloppy and inconsistent.

Singer and writer Joe Jackson, an outspoken defender of smokers' rights, observes that:

> 147 studies have been done on Secondhand Smoke [SHS] (also known as "passive smoking" or Environmental Tobacco Smoke, or ETS). Many of them are ridiculously flawed, since exposure to, and the effects of, SHS are extremely hard to measure. . . . The vast majority of studies (including the biggest and most credible ones) are inconclusive; i.e.; they show both positive and negative effects from SHS, do not reveal any consistent pattern, and have to be "thrown out." Only 24 studies have managed to show a "statistically significant" risk . . . but it's important to realize that *the risks are still so small they would not be taken seriously in any normal scientific context.* Your backyard barbecue produces far more carcinogens."[14]

The methodology behind the estimates of secondhand smoke fatalities is even more dubious, critics say. Such claims rely on meta-analysis, in which the results of various studies are combined into common-denominator terms and turned into a unified result. Among those who dispute the EPA claim is the science-fiction novelist Michael Crichton. Referring to studies on which the EPA relied, Crichton says, "This was openly fraudulent science, but it formed the basis for bans on smoking in restaurants, offices, and airports. . . . Soon, no claim was too extreme. . . . The American Cancer Society announced that 53,000 people died each year of second-hand smoke. The evidence for this claim is nonexistent."[15]

Critics such as Crichton further accuse regulatory agencies and public-policy think tanks of seeking to promote an antismoking agenda by simply ignoring studies that contradict the idea that secondhand smoke causes harm. One such study, by a pair of university-based public health researchers, looked at more than 100,000 Californians' exposure to secondhand smoke and came to the following conclusions:

The results do not support a causal relation between environmental tobacco smoke and tobacco related mortality, although they do not rule out a small effect. The association between exposure to environmental tobacco smoke and coronary heart disease and lung cancer may be considerably weaker than generally believed.[16]

Critics charge that instead of taking such findings into account, anti-smoking groups and government agencies select only the data that support the conclusion they want. Referring to an instance of such argumentation, critic Martha Perske writes that the study's authors claim that:

There is "robust epidemiologic evidence" implicating environmental tobacco smoke as a cause of lung cancer in nonsmokers. It appears, however, that in this case, "robust" evidence is little more than cherry-picked evidence. Misleading and selective data are presented. Results that are inconsistent with the desired position (banning smoking) are simply excluded.[17]

Such criticisms have not deterred the medical establishment or policy makers from concluding that secondhand smoke is dangerous. Perhaps the most definitive statement to date came in June 2006, when the U.S. surgeon general, the chief public health official in the nation, issued a report declaring unequivocally that secondhand smoke is a health hazard:

Today massive and conclusive scientific evidence documents adverse effects of involuntary smoking on children and adults, including cancer and cardiovascular diseases in adults, and adverse respiratory effects in both children and adults.[18]

This was not the first time a U.S. surgeon general had addressed secondhand smoke, but it was one of the most forceful. The report states that only a ban on smoking in indoor spaces fully protects nonsmokers from exposure to secondhand smoke. "Separating smokers from non-smokers, cleaning the air, and ventilating buildings cannot eliminate exposures of nonsmokers to secondhand smoke,"[19] the report says.

In remarks accompanying the release of the report, Surgeon General Richard H. Carmona pressed the point that no safe level of exposure to secondhand smoke has been established:

> We know that secondhand smoke harms people's health, but many people assume that exposure to secondhand smoke in small doses does not do any significant damage to one's health. However, science has proven that there is *no* risk-free level of exposure to secondhand smoke. Let me say that again: there is no safe level of exposure to secondhand smoke.[20]

Action to Curb Exposure

In any event, as far as policy makers are concerned, the debate seems to be over. There is a broad and accelerating trend toward banning smoking in places where the public may be exposed to what the surgeon general terms involuntary smoking.

Twelve states and numerous localities have enacted bans on smoking in public places, including privately owned public accommodations, such as bars and restaurants, though most laws provide some exceptions for adult-only establishments. Americans for Non-Smokers' Rights estimates that 39 percent of Americans now live in smoking-restricted localities. The group reports that at least 159 communities have enacted local restrictions on smoking.

> " There is a broad and accelerating trend toward banning smoking in places where the public may be exposed to what the surgeon general terms involuntary smoking. "

The federal government has also intervened to protect non-smokers. A 1997 executive order signed by President Bill Clinton banned smoking at all federal facilities. Federal law now banned smoking on domestic flights, and most airports have eliminated all indoor smoking.

The private sector is rapidly moving to curb smoking as well. Many employers have limited or banned tobacco use in workplaces. Their motives range from concern for workdays lost due to smokers' ill health to concerns about liability for nonsmokers who are exposed to tobacco smoke.

The Global Picture

Internationally, the situation is rather different. Relatively few countries have acted to protect the public against environmental tobacco smoke, and no clear pattern, either geographic or economic, exists among those that have. The countries that have acted most vigorously to curb public smoking are Bhutan, Ireland, Norway, Sweden, Italy, and New Zealand. Thailand has banned tobacco advertising and made moves to limit public exposure to smoke. Britain has a mixed response. Scotland has banned smoking in public places; England has yet to do so, although legislation is in place to restrict smoking starting in 2007. In the rest of Europe, restrictive legislation has had little effect—antismoking laws are widely ignored, even by some public entities, such as airports. The most conspicuous laxity, however, is in China, where smoking is rampant. With one-fifth of the world's population, China accounts for nearly one-third of all cigarette consumption. Unless Asian giants such as China and major European nations such as France get serious about restricting exposure to tobacco smoke, there will be no global momentum toward protecting the public from secondhand smoke.

In the United States, however, the trend appears irreversible. Some concerns about secondhand smoke may still be contestable in the scientific arena, but it appears that leaders in the medical and political establishments agree that it represents a genuine hazard. As the quotation by Philip Morris at the beginning of this chapter indicates, even some tobacco companies have thrown in the towel on secondhand smoke. Moreover, American social attitudes toward smoking have become far less tolerant than in the past. The current situation in America is best summed up by a bumper sticker that is popular among harried smokers: "At least I can still smoke in my car!" Even that, however, may not be true if there is a child aboard.

How Dangerous Is Exposure to Secondhand Smoke?

66 There is *no* risk-free level of secondhand smoke exposure, with even brief exposure adversely affecting the cardiovascular and respiratory system. 99

—Richard H. Carmona, "Remarks at Press Conference to Launch *Health Consequences of Involuntary Exposure to Tobacco Smoke: A Report of the Surgeon General*," June 27, 2006. www.surgeongeneral.gov.

Carmona became the 17th surgeon general of the U.S. Public Health Service on August 5, 2002.

66 It is impossible for SHS [secondhand smoke] to be a public health issue for the simple reason there is no proof that SHS has hurt anyone. 99

—Robert Hayes Halfpenny, "The Ten Biggest Lies About Smoke & Smoking," The Smoker's Club, Inc., 2005. www. smokersclubinc.com.

Halfpenny serves as vice president of Minnesotans Against Smoking Bans.

66 Don't even bring cigarettes into the house. . . . If there's any smoking in the home, kids suffer. 99

—Aviva Patz, "Boost Your Child's Health," *Parenting*, December/January 2004, p. 100.

Patz is a contributing editor for *Health* magazine.

* Editor's Note: While the definition of a primary source can be narrowly or broadly defined, for the purposes of Compact Research, a primary source consists of: 1) results of original research presented by an organization or researcher; 2) eyewitness accounts of events, personal experience, or work experience; 3) first-person editorials offering pundits' opinions; 4) government officials presenting political plans and/or policies; 5) representatives of organizations presenting testimony or policy.

66 Compelling evidence indicates that secondhand smoke is a health hazard. And it's nearly as bad as smoking itself. 99

—Mayo Clinic, "Secondhand Smoke: Avoid Dangers in the Air You Breathe," March 8, 2006. www.mayoclinic.com.

The Mayo Clinic, based in Rochester, Minnesota, is a world-renowned medical treatment and research facility.

66 Common sense should have put this into the garbage pail. If secondhand smoke killed, we'd all be dead. 99

—Sidney Zion, "Judge Smokes Out Tobacco Lie," *New York Daily News*, July 23, 1998. www.junkscience.com.

Zion is an opinion columnist for the *New York Daily News*.

66 ETS [environmental tobacco smoke] has a number of serious impacts on children's health, including sudden infant death syndrome (SIDS) . . . asthma, increased respiratory tract infections, increased middle ear infections, and . . . developmental toxicity resulting in low birth weight and impaired lung function. 99

—California Air Resources Board, "Proposed Identification of Environmental Tobacco Smoke as a Toxic Air Contaminant, as Approved by the Scientific Review Panel," Appendix III, June 24, 2005, p. 10. ftp://ftp.arb.ca.gov.

The California Air Resources Board is a government organization created by the California Assembly in 1967 to maintain healthy air quality in the state.

66 Statistically, you are much more likely to die in a bicycle accident, or from being left-handed and using right-handed things, than from exposure to smoke. (I swear I'm not making this up!) 99

—Joe Jackson, "The Smoking Issue," 2004. www.forestonline.org.

Jackson has been a classical performer, punk rocker, and swing musician. He also writes nonfiction essays on smoking and other subjects.

"The more we learn about the dangers of secondhand smoke the more unacceptable it becomes for anyone to be exposed to these hazards in order to earn a paycheck or go out to a restaurant or bar."

—Matthew L. Myers, "New Study Adds to Evidence Smoke-Free Laws Reduce Heart Attacks, Shows Need to Make All Workplaces Smoke-Free," Tobacco-Free Kids, September 6, 2006. www.tobaccofreekids.org.

Myers is president of the Campaign for Tobacco-Free Kids. An attorney by training, he previously headed up the Federal Trade Commission's monitoring of tobacco advertising.

"Surely, if we can agree that children and teenagers should not smoke, we can also agree that they should also not be exposed to secondhand smoke."

—Carol M. Browner, U.S. Senate Committee on Environment & Public Works, "Environmental Tobacco Smoke Issues Relative to the June 20 Agreement," April 1, 1998. http://epw.senate.gov.

Browner was administrator of the Environmental Protection Agency during the Clinton administration.

"The social norms are changing. It's no longer OK to blow smoke in someone's face."

— Annie Tegen, quoted in Wendy Koch, "39% Live in Areas Limiting Smoking," *USA Today,* December 28, 2005. www.usatoday.com.

Tegen is spokeswoman for the civic group Americans for Non-Smokers' Rights.

"The risk of secondary smoke to nonsmokers has been twisted and exaggerated beyond all reason purely as a tool of social engineering."

—Michael McFadden, Author's Preface, *Dissecting Antismokers' Brains.* www.antibrains.com.

McFadden is the author of *Dissecting Antismokers' Brains.* He lives in Philadelphia.

66 Nonsmoking spouses are exposed to the poisons and carcinogens in smoke, and their chances for long-term disease and death are, therefore, greatly increased. Parents need to understand that smoking in the home may lead young infants and children toward acute and chronic respiratory problems. 99

—American Nurses Association, "Environmental Tobacco Smoke," December 12, 1997. www.nursingworld.org.

The American Nurses Association (ANA) represents the nation's nearly 3 million registered nurses. Among other activities, the ANA advances the nursing profession by lobbying on health-care issues affecting nurses and the public.

66 [The surgeon general's 2006] report [on secondhand smoke] should be a wake-up call for lawmakers to enact comprehensive clean indoor air laws that prohibit smoking in all indoor public places and workplaces. 99

—Ron Davis, Statement on surgeon general's report on secondhand smoke, June 27, 2006. www.amaassn.org.

Davis is president-elect of the American Medical Association. A doctor and epidemiologist, he is also director of the Center for Health Promotion and Disease Prevention at the Henry Ford Health System in Detroit.

66 Americans know all too well how many young men and women this country lost in the entire Vietnam War. We lose almost that many every year to secondhand smoke! Fifty-three thousand nonsmokers die each year from exposure to environmental tobacco smoke! 99

—Carla Stovall, U.S. Senate Committee on Environment & Public Works, "Environmental Tobacco Smoke Issues Relative to the June 20 Agreement," April 1, 1998. http://epw.senate.gov.

Stovall was the attorney general of Kansas at the time she gave the congressional testimony from which this quotation is drawn.

How Dangerous Is Exposure to Secondhand Smoke?

- Secondhand smoke contains more than 40 known carcinogens.

- The U.S. Environmental Protection Agency estimates that 3,000 thousand nonsmokers a year die from lung cancer caused by second-hand smoke.

- The Centers for Disease Control and Prevention estimate that exposure to secondhand smoke kills approximately 46,000 Americans a year by aggravating coronary heart disease.

- The effect of secondhand smoke on children is worst during a child's first five years.

- According to the U.S. surgeon general, there is credible scientific evidence that secondhand smoke is a cause of sudden infant death syndrome.

- Secondhand smoke is responsible for up to 300,000 lung illnesses, such as pneumonia and bronchitis, in infants and young children each year.

- Children living in households with smokers are more likely to have a buildup of fluid in their middle ear, which is an indication of chronic middle ear disease.

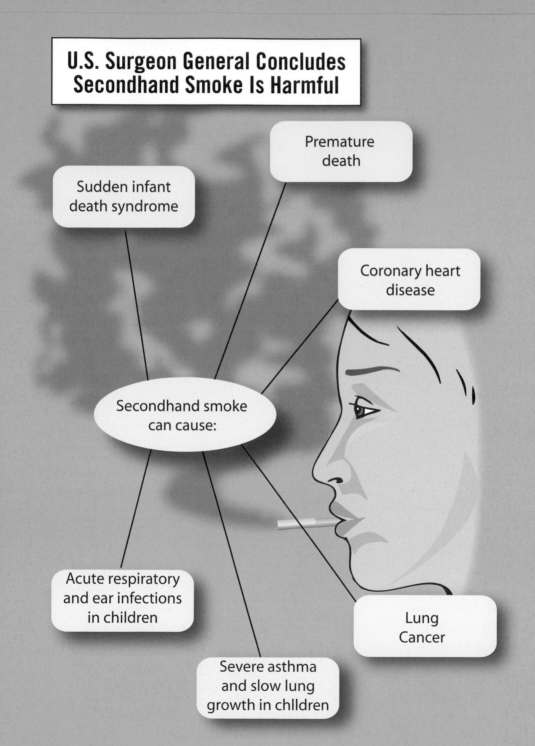

U.S. Surgeon General Concludes Secondhand Smoke Is Harmful

Premature death

Sudden infant death syndrome

Coronary heart disease

Secondhand smoke can cause:

Acute respiratory and ear infections in children

Lung Cancer

Severe asthma and slow lung growth in chlldren

Source: U.S. Surgeon General, *The Health Consequences of Involuntary Exposure to Tobacco Smoke,* June 27, 2006.

- The U.S. surgeon general has declared that scientific evidence indicates that there is no risk-free level of exposure to secondhand smoke.

- A nonsmoker's risk of contracting lung cancer rises by 23 percent if he or she is exposed over the long term to secondhand smoke from his or her spouse, according to an international study published in 2004.

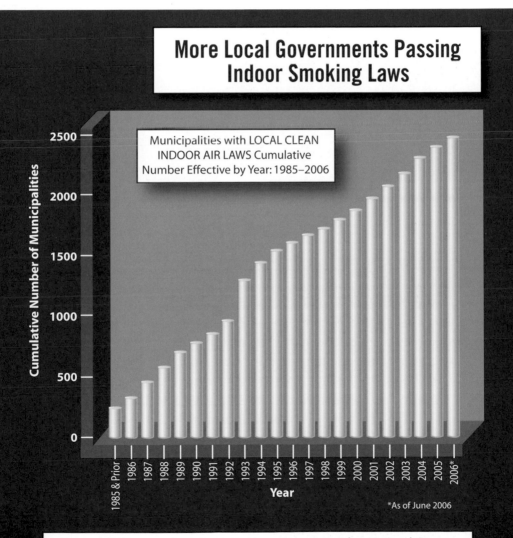

More Local Governments Passing Indoor Smoking Laws

Municipalities with LOCAL CLEAN INDOOR AIR LAWS Cumulative Number Effective by Year: 1985–2006

*As of June 2006

Since 1985 more local governments across the United States have been passing laws against indoor smoking. The number of municipalities with such legislation has increased over 1,000 percent to 2,306 municipalities in 2006.

Source: American Nonsmokers' Rights Foundation, July 1, 2006. www.no-smoke.org.

51

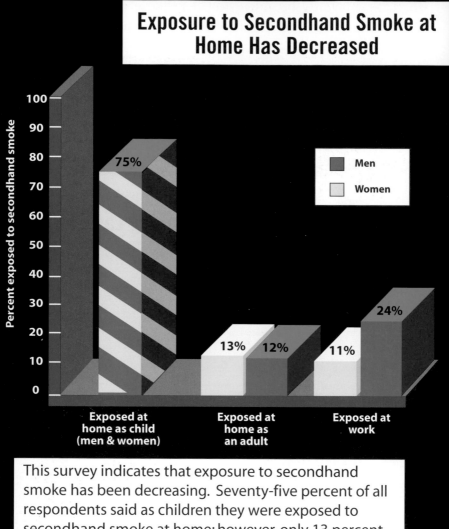

Exposure to Secondhand Smoke at Home Has Decreased

Percent exposed to secondhand smoke

- Men
- Women

75%

13% 12%

11% 24%

Exposed at home as child (men & women)

Exposed at home as an adult

Exposed at work

This survey indicates that exposure to secondhand smoke has been decreasing. Seventy-five percent of all respondents said as children they were exposed to secondhand smoke at home; however, only 13 percent of women and 12 percent of men said they are currently exposed to secondhand smoke at home.

Source: Archives of Internal Medicine, October 9, 2006.

- Twelve states have enacted restrictions on exposure to secondhand smoke in public places. The federal government has banned smoking on commercial airline flights and in most federal facilities.

- As of late 2006, 168 countries had signed an international treaty committing them to restrict smoking.

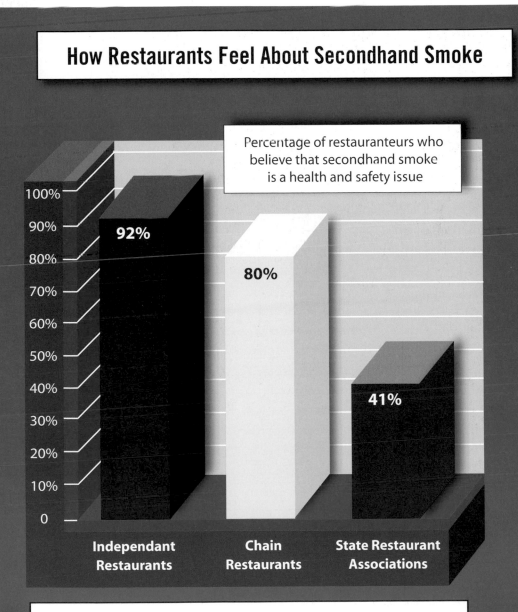

How Restaurants Feel About Secondhand Smoke

Percentage of restauranteurs who believe that secondhand smoke is a health and safety issue

92% — Independant Restaurants

80% — Chain Restaurants

41% — State Restaurant Associations

Restaurant operators' opinion on the health impact of secondhand smoke varies based on the type of operator. Ninety-two percent of independent operators believe secondhand smoke is a health issue, compared with 80 percent of chain operators and only 41 percent of state restaurant associations.

Source: Kids Involuntary Inhaling Second-Hand Smoke (KIISS), 2002. www.kiiss.org.

Why Do Many Young People Smoke or Chew Tobacco?

"Every day in the U.S., 2,000 teens become newly addicted to smoking. Think about it: most will not be able to quit for 17 years, and over 800 of those teens will later die from cigarettes."

—Patrick Reynolds, grandson of tobacco company founder R.J. Reynolds, undated.

Ever since U.S. surgeon general Luther Terry's 1964 report linking tobacco and cancer, the federal government has constantly warned of the dangers of smoking. Today, even the tobacco companies concede that their product is dangerous. Yet tobacco use in America persists, especially among young people.

Youths constitute the one segment of the population that is largely indifferent to risk. Though there are exceptions, on average adolescents are more inclined to take risks and less likely to weigh long-term risks than are adults. Another factor contributing to teen tobacco use is easy accessibility. In many states, it continues to be relatively easy for underage persons to buy cigarettes or other tobacco products. Even when such products are locked away, access is possible if a parent, older sibling, or other adult smoker lives in the teen's household. Finally, and perhaps most fundamentally, the risks involved in smoking actually add to its sex appeal, which for teenagers is a powerful incentive. Researchers call this the "forbidden fruit" syndrome.

With these facts in mind, it may come as no surprise that 80 percent of smokers begin smoking by the age of 18. Surveys show that currently half of all teenagers try tobacco by the end of high school and that about a quarter become regular users.

The primary reason why adolescents try tobacco appears to be marketing. Yet, once they begin to experiment, the nicotine in tobacco becomes the principal reason why many stay with it.

The effect of marketing on youth is evident in the historical records of smoking patterns. As with adults, the prevalence of smoking among American teens peaked in 1976, when about 40 percent of all teens (and roughly 50 percent of adults) smoked. Thereafter, smoking rates began to fall for all age groups. However, beginning in 1990, a resurgence of tobacco use began among American teens. It topped out in 1997, by which time an estimated 35 percent of 12th graders were smokers, with boys and girls getting hooked in equal proportions. Specialized marketing aimed at youth by the tobacco companies is widely seen as the cause.

> " The primary reason why adolescents try tobacco appears to be marketing. "

During that period, tobacco companies spent vast amounts of money to market their products to young people. By the end of the decade, companies were collectively spending approximately $10 billion a year on advertising and promotions, much of it aimed squarely at youth through magazines with young subscribers, sponsorship of sporting events favored by the young, and product placement in entertainment. That made tobacco one of the most heavily advertised products in the marketplace.

The principal figure in the 1990s advertising efforts was the now-defunct Joe Camel, focus of a campaign initiated by the R.J. Reynolds Tobacco Company. The cartoon character became the icon of a young, hip, and rebellious generation of smokers. A 1986 Reynolds company memo shows that young males were the target of the campaign. In particular, it set the goal of repositioning Camel cigarettes to appeal to males 18 to 24 years old. This was to be achieved by conveying the idea that to smoke Camels was to appear masculine, self-confident, and non-conformist. Critics charge that the company was marketing to an even younger audience.

That Joe Camel made a deep impression on young people is beyond dispute. A study published in the *Journal of the American Medical Association* shows that more than 90 percent of six-year-olds could identify Joe

Camel and connect him with cigarettes. Only Mickey Mouse was more widely recognized.

Joe Camel was a runaway success, accounting for much of the rise in youth smoking during the 1990s. There were other youth marketing ploys, however. The tobacco industry, always in search of new customers, stepped up its advertising aimed at young women. Following the initial success of Virginia Slims, the first cigarette marketed specifically to women, other female-oriented tobacco products followed. According to the American Heart Association:

> One of the most egregious examples of the tobacco industry's targeting of women was the introduction of 'Dakota' [cigarettes] by R.J. Reynolds in 1990. An internal Reynolds marketing plan revealed that Dakota was to be marketed to 'virile females' between the ages of 18 and 24 who have no education beyond high school and who watch soap operas and attend tractor pulls.[21]

Such targeted marketing paid off. During the 1990s, smoking among girls and young women shot up. From 1991 to 1999 high-school girls who smoked increased from 27 to 35 percent.

Things changed in 1998, when a landmark legal case resulted in the Master Settlement Agreement (MSA), which forced tobacco companies to drop advertising campaigns deemed to be aimed at youth. After the demise of Joe Camel and other youth-oriented advertising gimmicks, a counter-advertising campaign, funded by tobacco companies forced by the MSA, took hold. The ads, many of them created by young people, drove down youth smoking rates. So, too, did other measures, such as increased penalties for selling tobacco to minors and higher taxes on the product. From 1997 to 2001, a series of tax hikes pushed the price of cigarettes up by about 70 percent. Smoking among teenagers fell fast, by 30 percent according to various surveys. Nevertheless, a substantial number of American teens continue to light up or chew tobacco. Current estimates of youthful smokers range from 22 to 25 percent, while estimates of boys who use smokeless or chewing tobacco range from 6 to 10 percent, with girls hovering at about 1 percent. Whatever the exact number, experts agree that the percentage of young people who smoke is now greater than the percentage of adults.

Meanwhile, the marketing of tobacco to youth continues in more subtle ways. Tobacco companies' advertising spending has not diminished. Product placement continues to be a key strategy. A 2005 study found that actors seen smoking in movies has a strong effect on teenage behavior. Since teens are the largest group of moviegoers, the influence is profound. Other marketing efforts involve retooling the product itself. Antismoking activists have blasted tobacco companies for introducing flavored cigarettes with names like "Mocha Taboo." These sweet, flavored products are an attempt to appeal to youths, critics charge.

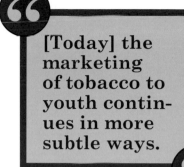

> [Today] the marketing of tobacco to youth continues in more subtle ways.

Smokeless Tobacco

Smoking is not the only way that youngsters use tobacco. Since 1970, according to the Campaign for Tobacco-Free Kids, smokeless tobacco has gone from a product used primarily by older men to one used predominantly by young men and boys. The product, also known as snuff, spit, or chewing tobacco, is consumed by placing a pinch or wad in the mouth, between cheek and gums.

In 1970 males 65 and older were almost 6 times as likely as young men to use smokeless tobacco regularly. By 1991, however, young males were 50 percent more likely than older ones to be regular users. Despite some recent declines in youth smokeless-tobacco use, as many as 10 percent of boys in U.S. high schools and just over 1 percent of high-school girls currently use smokeless-tobacco products.

Although these products do not produce smoke, they are addictive and hazardous. Smokeless tobacco causes oral lesions on the cheeks, gums, and tongue and can lead to oral cancer. Studies have found that up to 78 percent of smokeless-tobacco users have oral lesions. Other dangers lurk in its use as well. Among these are rotting teeth, throat and stomach cancer, and heart disease.

The rise in smokeless-tobacco use among young people has been attributed to the same causes as the rise in youth smoking—direct and indirect marketing. The direct marketing involves ads and logos at sporting events, such as car races. The indirect marketing involved celebrities, especially athletes, who are shown using the products.

Youth Suffer Various Harms

Some people mistakenly believe that the effects of smoking only show up in late middle age. This is not true. Although sometimes subtly, tobacco use nevertheless affects teenagers right from the start. It can impede the rate of lung growth and the level of maximum lung function. Regular smoking causes frequent coughing in young people and leads to increased respiratory illnesses. It hampers young people's physical fitness in terms of both performance and endurance—even among young people trained in competitive running. Smoking also affects the heart early on. The resting heart rate of a young adult smoker averages 2 to 3 beats per minute faster than that of a typical nonsmoker. In sum, studies show that teens who smoke are 2.4 times more likely than their nonsmoking peers to report poor overall health.

> Some people mistakenly believe that the effects of smoking only show up in late middle age.

Among the many causes for concern about youth smoking is that it is often a gateway to other risky behaviors. According to the U.S. Centers for Disease Control and Prevention, teens who smoke are 3 times more likely than nonsmokers to use alcohol, 8 times more likely to use marijuana, and 22 times more likely to use cocaine. Smoking is also associated with a host of other risky behaviors, such as fighting and engaging in unprotected sex. No one would argue that tobacco is a direct cause of these risky behaviors, but the correlation is extremely important all the same. The reason is that teens, even more than adults, are susceptible to influence by their peers. Teenagers tend to segregate themselves into cliques, and one of the important demarcation lines is between smokers and nonsmokers. In other words, if young adults get in with a group whose members are smokers, he or she is far more likely to be exposed to the risky and often illegal behaviors listed above than if a group of nonsmokers is chosen.

The Decline in Teen Smoking May Be Ending

The substantial decrease in smoking rates among teenagers since 1997 has encouraged many Americans to think that the epidemic of youth smoking has been permanently extinguished, but that may not be so. In late 2005 researchers at the University of Michigan sounded a warning: "We are still seeing some residual declines in smoking in the upper grades, as the lower-smoking birth cohorts make their way up the age spectrum," said Lloyd Johnston, the study's principal investigator. "But even in the upper grades a slowdown is occurring, and we believe the declines are likely to end very soon."[22]

A major reason for the slowdown in smoking reduction is a decline in antitobacco advertising aimed at youth, the study found. "Insofar as these antismoking ad campaigns have had their intended effects—and there is growing evidence that they have—the pullback that is now occurring in the funding of such campaigns at both the national and state levels is not a favorable development," [23] Johnston concluded.

Critics of smoking charge that tobacco companies are once again encouraging youth to smoke. This time, they say, it is not through direct advertising (which remains banned under the 1998 Master Settlement Agreement), but rather through more subtle means. One is the introduction of discount cigarettes, which have largely offset the tobacco tax increases that many states implemented to discourage youth smoking. Tobacco companies vigorously deny this. They point to their youth-smoking prevention programs as evidence that they have completely ended any role in marketing to youth. However, some critics even charge that the tobacco companies' youth-smoking prevention programs actually promote smoking.

In a 2002 letter to the heads of three major tobacco companies, the presidents of the International Union Against Cancer, the International Union Against Tuberculosis and Lung Disease, and the World Heart Federation characterized the youth tobacco prevention programs as a "deceit" that should be halted "without further delay."[24]

Whichever side is right, the fact remains that millions of American youth smoke or use smokeless tobacco, and a reduction in prevalence of tobacco use among youth has slowed and may be stalling. Once young people start using tobacco, they rarely quit in less than a decade. Some are never able to give it up. It is clear, therefore, that the challenge of preventing young people from getting hooked on nicotine has not ended and will likely continue well into the future.

Why Do Many Young People Smoke or Chew Tobacco?

❝ [Advertising] will leverage the nonconformist, self-confident mindset historically attributed to the CAMEL user to address smokers' desire to project an image that elevates them in the eyes of their peers.**❞**

—R.J. Reynolds Tobacco Company internal memo, "Camel New Advertising Campaign," March 12, 1986. www.the smokinggun.com.

This extract is from a memo that laid out the strategy leading to the Joe Camel advertising campaign. It is one of thousands of tobacco company documents that became public in the course of litigation.

....

❝ If you're really, really not going to sell to children, they're not going to have any customers in 25 or 30 years.**❞**

—Bennett S. LeBow, *Frontline* Online, "Inside the Tobacco Deal: Interviews: Bennett LeBow," PBS, undated. www. pbs.org.

LeBow is the chief executive officer of the Brooke Group, which owns Liggett Tobacco, the smallest of the six major tobacco companies. He was the first to settle with state attorneys general in their lawsuit over the harm caused by tobacco.

....

* Editor's Note: While the definition of a primary source can be narrowly or broadly defined, for the purposes of Compact Research, a primary source consists of: 1) results of original research presented by an organization or researcher; 2) eyewitness accounts of events, personal experience, or work experience; 3) first-person editorials offering pundits' opinions; 4) government officials presenting political plans and/or policies; 5) representatives of organizations presenting testimony or policy.

66 Defendants [the major tobacco companies] have consistently made false and misleading statements that their expenditures on advertising and marketing were directed exclusively at convincing current smokers to switch brands, not at enticing children. 99

—Gladys Kessler, "Memorandum Opinion," *United States v. Philip Morris et al.* September 28, 2000. www.usdoj.gov.

Kessler is a federal judge in the U.S. District Court for the District of Columbia.

66 Smoking in movies is a risk factor for smoking initiation among US adolescents. Limiting exposure of young adolescents to movie smoking could have important public health implications. 99

—James D. Sargent et al., "Exposure to Movie Smoking: Its Relation to Smoking Initiation Among US Adolescents," *Pediatrics.* vol. 116, no. 5, November 2005. http://pediatrics.aappublications.org.

Sargent is a physician who serves as an associate professor of pediatrics in the Dartmouth-Hitchcock Medical Center in New Hampshire.

66 To maintain business growth, tobacco companies need to initiate thousands of new smokers every day. Hence, children frequently are exposed to tobacco ads in stores, on billboards and in certain sports, entertainment and teen-oriented magazines. 99

—Sarah M. Greene, "Alcohol, Tobacco Campaigns Frequently Aimed at Women, Children and Minorities," IPRC Newsline, Spring 1992. www.drugs.indiana.edu.

Greene holds a master's degree in public health and serves as a research associate at the Center for Health Studies in Seattle, Washington.

❝If you took 1,000 young adult smokers, one will be murdered, six will die on the roads, but 500 will die from tobacco.❞

—Richard Peto, quoted in "The Burden of Tobacco Use," *Absolute Advantage*, 2006, p. 24. www.welcoa.org.

Peto is a professor of medical statistics and epidemiology at Oxford University in England. He is a leader in the field of meta-analysis on cancer studies, allowing different studies to be combined for an overall result.

❝We know smoking tobacco is not good for kids, but a lot of other things aren't good. Drinking's not good. Some would say milk's not good.❞

—Bob Dole, quoted in SCARC Action Alert, "Presidential Nominee Dole Questions Smoking's Addictiveness, Danger; National Attention Turns to Tobacco Money in Politics," July 31, 1996. www.tobacco.org.

Dole, a former U.S. senator from Kansas, was majority leader of the Senate from 1995 until 1996, when he became the Republican Party's candidate for president.

❝We overlook the fact that anti-tobacco doctors and activists, who advocate teenagers use nicotine through 'Smoke Free' delivery methods, are teaching our kids in the classroom. Drug companies don't need to advertise near schools, their activists are discreetly promoting 'Tobacco Free' nicotine patches, gums and inhalers face-to-face with kids in the classroom.❞

—Norman E. Kjono, "Targeting Kids for Drugs," FORCES, April 14, 1998. www.forces.org.

Kjono is a member of the board of directors of FORCES, a smokers' advocacy group that disparages the motives of organizations against youth smoking.

66 Tobacco companies selling cigarettes like pineapple and coconut-flavored 'Kauai Kolada' and 'Midnight Berry' is an attempt to market to youth, in my opinion. Even for the tobacco industry, this marketing gimmick is beyond the pale. 99

—Tim Pawlenty, quoted in Office of Governor Tim Pawlenty, "Governor Pawlenty Proposes Banning Specialty and Candy Flavored Cigarettes in Minnesota," February 10, 2005. www.governor.state.mn.us.

Pawlenty, governor of Minnesota, in 2005 became the nation's first state leader to propose legislation to ban the sale of flavored cigarettes.

66 I would say that the most common reason though is that kids who smoke often begin smoking to fit in with a peer group who thinks that smoking is cool. Of course, once kids get hooked, they smoke because they crave smoking and find it very difficult to stop. 99

—Michael H. Popkin, "Dr. Popkin Interviews," Keep Kids from Smoking.com, undated. www.keepkidsfromsmoking. com.

Popkin founded Active Parenting Publishers in 1983. His video-based parenting education program, *Active Parenting*, has been used by millions of parents to improve their skills in raising their children.

66 We were getting new replacement smokers and we, in our minds, were told to recruit 13–14 year old boys. 99

—David Goerlitz, cited in "Quotations from *Tobacco Wars*, 1999. www.ash.org.

Goerlitz is a professional actor, producer, and public speaker. Once best known for his role as the "Winston Man" in cigarette commercials, he has become an antismoking advocate.

"Tobacco companies have been aggressively targeting Latinos, especially Latino youth, resulting in increased smoking and increasingly severe health damage to the Latino community."

—Guillermo Brito, quoted in National Latino Council on Alcohol and Tobacco Prevention, "Letter to Aníbal Acevedo Vilá, Governor of Puerto Rico," August 23, 2005. www.nlcatp.org.

Brito is executive director of the National Latino Council on Alcohol and Tobacco Prevention.

"Although the recent decreases in smoking have more than offset the substantial rise in teen smoking during the early 1990s, the current rates are still far higher than parents and the public health community would like to see. And considerable evidence is accumulating that the downturn in teen smoking may stall at about these still unacceptable levels."

—Lloyd Johnston, quoted in Joe Serwach, "Teen Smoking Rates and Illicit Drug Use Continue to Drop," *University Record* Online, January 3, 2006. www.umich.edu.

Johnston is the principal investigator of the Monitoring the Future study of youth behavior. He is a psychologist and research professor at the University of Michigan's Institute for Social Research.

Facts and Illustrations

Why Do Many Young People Smoke or Chew Tobacco?

- Each day in the United States, approximately 3,000 youngsters between the ages of 12 and 17 try their first cigarette.

- More than 80 percent of people who smoke start smoking between the ages of 12 and 18.

- Fifty-four percent of high-school students in America have tried smoking a cigarette at least once.

- Young people who smoke generally experience more health problems in their teens than those who do not, especially respiratory problems.

- The younger the smoker, the swifter and stronger the addiction to nicotine generally is.

- After a rise from 1991 to 1997, cigarette smoking among youths has fallen, showing a very large and statistically significant downward trend since 1999.

- In 2003 approximately 22 percent of all American teens were cigarette smokers, and another 6 percent used tobacco in some other form, such as cigars or chewing tobacco.

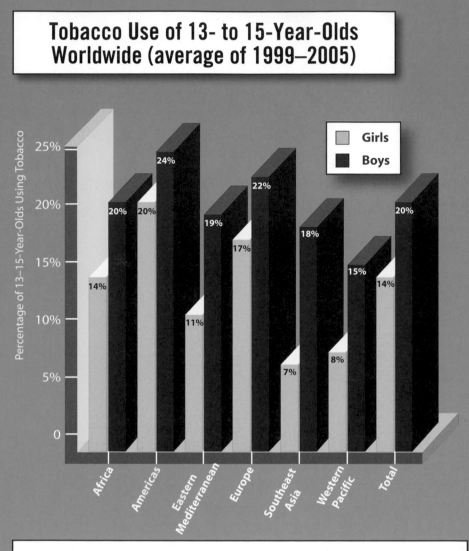

Tobacco Use of 13- to 15-Year-Olds Worldwide (average of 1999–2005)

This chart indicates that from 1999–2005, tobacco use by 13- to 15-year-olds was highest in the Americas at 22 percent. In all the world regions, use was higher among boys than girls.

Source: Centers for Disease Control and Prevention, *Morbidity and Mortality Weekly Report*, May 26, 2006. www.cdc.gov.

- The gender difference in cigarette smoking has greatly narrowed among U.S. high-school students: 25 percent of boys and 21 percent of girls smoke, according to the U.S. Department of Health and Human Services.

- In 2003 cigarette companies spent $15.2 billion on advertising and promotion of their products, equivalent to $340 for each adult smoker in America.

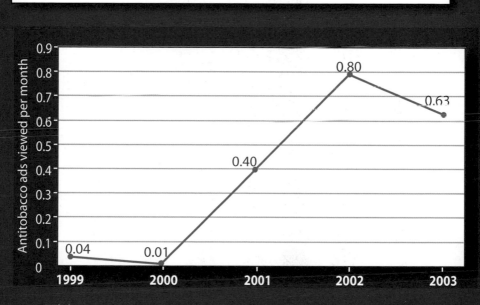

Estimated Teen Exposure to Antitobacco TV Ads per Month (37 States*)

*Alabama, Arizona, Arkansas, California, Colorado, Connecticut, Florida, Georgia, Hawaii, Illinois, Indiana, Iowa, Kansas, Kentucky, Louisiana, Maryland, Massachusetts, Michigan, Minnesota, Missouri, Nebraska, Nevada, New Mexico, New York, North Carolina, Ohio, Oklahoma, Oregon, Pennsylvania, South Carolina, Tennessee, Texas, Utah, Virginia, Washington, West Virginia, and Wisconsin.

This graph shows the average number of antitobacco television advertisements that 12- to 17-year-olds viewed each month in 37 states from 1999 to 2003. As state funding for antitobacco advertising increased from 2000 to 2002, teens were exposed to nearly one advertisement each month in 2002. The decline from 2002 to 2003 reflects the decrease in funding for antitobacco advertising.

Source: Centers for Disease Control and Prevention, *Morbidity and Mortality Weekly Report*, October 28, 2005.

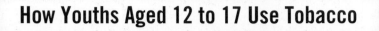

How Youths Aged 12 to 17 Use Tobacco

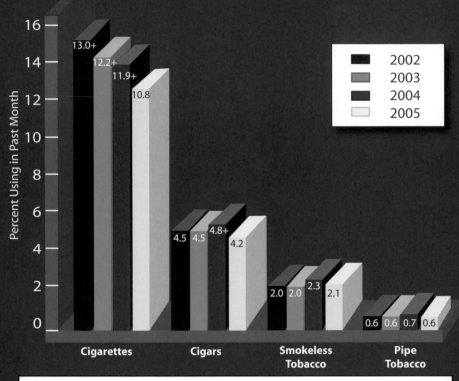

Teenage cigarette consumption decreased from 2002 to 2005, but use of cigars, smokeless tobacco, and pipe tobacco remained relatively unchanged. Some experts warn, however, that recent decreases in funding for antitobacco advertising will cause teenage tobacco usage to increase.

Source: Department of Health and Human Services, Substance Abuse and Mental Health Services Administration, 2006.

- The most heavily advertised cigarette brands—Marlboro, Newport, and Camel—are also the ones most popular with smokers aged 12 to 17.

How Can Nicotine and Tobacco Use Be Reduced?

> **&&What we need to do is to prevent kids from ever be-coming addicted to nicotine.&&**
>
> — U.S. Food and Drug Administration commissioner David Kessler.

Experts agree that the reduction of tobacco use can best be achieved by preventing people from ever getting involved with the substance in the first place. Above all else, that means stopping the marketing of tobacco to youth; however, assisting and encouraging those who are already addicted is important, too. The strategies for each goal are somewhat different, but each involves difficult questions of balancing individual freedoms and corporate rights with the common good. Attempts to reduce tobacco use through prevention fall into several categories: restrictions on marketing, public education, school-based prevention programs, controlling access, and tax policies.

Battles over Marketing

Few people start using tobacco once they are out of their teens, so experts agree that youth must be protected from tobacco advertising and promotion. Efforts to do so have a long and tangled history. In 1971 the federal government banned all tobacco advertising from television. This presented a huge marketing obstacle to the industry, but tobacco firms proved ingenious at circumventing it.

Their chief strategy has been to sponsor events that appear on television. The year following the ban, Philip Morris, the largest of the tobacco companies, became the sponsor of the newly formed Women's Tennis

Association, whose tournament circuit came to bear the name of the company's recently introduced cigarette for women, Virginia Slims. Other sporting and cultural event sponsorships soon followed. The benefit to the industry was enormous.

Medical researcher Michael Siegel of the Boston University School of Public Health found that in the 1990s, when youth smoking shot up, tobacco companies increasingly used corporate sponsorship to market their wares. Despite the ban on television advertising, they were able to get their logos and slogans on the air, often for hours at a time. Siegel concludes that to "report tobacco company television advertising expenditures as zero is grossly inaccurate, and completely ignores the millions of dollars in television advertising value achieved through their sponsorship of motor sports events."[25]

Subsequently, tobacco companies, faced with a massive government lawsuit, agreed to limit their use of cigarette brand names in sponsorships. In particular, they said they would no longer sponsor any event in which people under the age of 18 were participants. Just as important, in the deal known as the Master Settlement Agreement (MSA), the industry agreed to halt all other forms of marketing to youth.

> "Antitobacco advocates ... claim that the companies continue to find ways to seduce youth into smoking.

Antitobacco advocates, however, claim that the companies continue to find ways to seduce youth into smoking. They note a 50 percent rise in cigarette marketing budgets in recent years. Aggregate spending on advertising and promotions by tobacco companies went from $10 billion in 2000 to a staggering $15.4 billion in 2005. Some of that money went into new media, such as subscription cable, satellite TV, and the Internet. More than 500 Web sites sell tobacco products, accounting for more than 10 percent of sales. Since young people are among the most enthusiastic users of the Web, finding ways to restrict online tobacco marketing will be crucial to reducing future nicotine addiction.

Starstruck

Not all the marketing is channeled through new media. Another key tobacco marketing strategy, critics claim, is to have Hollywood actors smoke during movies. A 2001 study published in the prestigious medical journal the *Lancet* claims that smoking scenes in movies jumped more than tenfold in the decade after a 1988 agreement that was meant to halt such product placements. The U.S. Centers for Disease Control and Prevention report that "after decades of decline, smoking in movies, which has been linked to youth smoking, increased rapidly beginning in the early 1990s and by 2002 was at levels observed in 1950."[26]

The depiction of smoking in movies is nearly always sensuous and attractive, and the fact that stars such as John Travolta and Julia Roberts are the ones doing the smoking makes a deep impression on many young viewers. "We have strong data [showing that] smoking in the movies encourages kids to smoke," [27] says Stanton Glantz, director of the University of California at San Francisco Center for Tobacco Control Research and Education.

Acknowledging the role of the entertainment media in promoting tobacco use, some celebrities have volunteered their time to combat smoking. Some of Hollywood's most powerful voices—including actors Ted Danson, Sean Penn, Rob Reiner, and model Christy Turlington—have banded together to make documentaries about the responsibility of celebrities and the hazards of portraying smoking as "cool."

Glantz proposes a more draconian solution. He wants the Motion Picture Association of America to slap an R rating on any movie that includes smoking. That way, no one under the age of 17 would be admitted without a parent. The World Health Organization has endorsed the proposal.

Some countries, such as Norway and Finland, have imposed complete prohibitions on tobacco advertising and sponsorships. If such a ban were proposed in the United States, however, it would certainly face constitutional challenges based on the First Amendment right to free speech. So long as tobacco remains a legal product, many experts say, the right to advertise it is protected.

Public Education

Nearly as important as curbs on tobacco marketing are efforts to educate the public—especially young people—about the reasons to avoid or quit using tobacco. Results of such efforts have been mixed. Ironically, the most direct attempt at deterrence has been the least effective. Since 1965 U.S.

law has required that cigarette packages carry a now-famous health warning: "Caution: Cigarette Smoking May Be Hazardous to Your Health." In 1984, after the Federal Trade Commission concluded that the original warning had had little effect, a new, more explicit set of warnings was issued. Among them was this: "SURGEON GENERAL'S WARNING: Smoking Causes Lung Cancer, Heart Disease, Emphysema, and May Complicate Pregnancy." Two years later, a similar warning was applied to smokeless tobacco, and eventually cigars came to bear surgeon general's warnings as well. Nevertheless, all such warning labels have proven virtually useless in deterring youth from purchasing tobacco. A 1997 Stanford University study concluded that "sizable proportions of adolescent smokers are not seeing, reading, or remembering cigarette warning labels. . . . The current warning labels are ineffective among adolescents."[28]

A very different approach grew out of the 1998 MSA. The tobacco companies' settlement with state attorneys general forced them to put up approximately $200 billion for tobacco prevention. A small portion of those funds went into creating and funding the American Legacy Foundation, dedicated to promoting the rejection of tobacco. Using its allocation of $300 million a year for 5 years, the foundation funded a number of aggressive new antismoking campaigns aimed at youth. The most notable of these is the "truth" tobacco education advertising campaign. Created by and for young people, the campaign aims to show the impact of tobacco in highly emotive ways. One of its most famous ads shows teenagers piling up 1,200 body bags outside the New York offices of a major tobacco company to dramatize the daily death toll of tobacco. Not content to remain in one medium, the truth campaign also launched ads on the Internet.

Norway and Finland . . . have imposed complete prohibitions on tobacco advertising and sponsorships.

The impact has been dramatic. According to a study published in June 2002 in the *American Journal of Public Health*, the percentage of kids ages 12 to 17 who were aware of any antitobacco campaign doubled during the first ten months of the truth campaign. More significant, the percentage of young people using tobacco fell dramatically. From a peak of 36 percent in 1997, youth smoking plummeted to 22 percent in 2003. Most experts believe that the hard-hitting media campaign with its edgy ads greatly contributed to that decline. One study attributes a third of the reduction in youth smoking to the truth campaign. Not everyone agrees on its effectiveness, though. Public health expert Joel M. Moskowitz notes that "the campaign's impact did not sustain through high school suggest[ing] that 'truth' advertising was no more effective than school-based smoking prevention programs."[29]

In any event, after 2003 funding for the American Legacy Foundation dropped by more than 80 percent, sapping much of its vitality. Coincidentally or not, the fall in teen smoking immediately stalled. The future of the truth campaign has been further imperiled by a tobacco company lawsuit that claims the ads went too far and vilified the tobacco industry.

Many tobacco control experts firmly assert, however, that a youth-led ad campaign is crucial to future reductions in tobacco use. In 2004 they banded together to form the Citizens' Commission to Protect the Truth. Its members include all living former U.S. secretaries of health, U.S. surgeons general, and directors of the U.S. Centers for Disease Control and Prevention (CDC). If they are to be believed, dramatic advertising about the dangers of tobacco will remain a crucial weapon in the battle to reduce smoking.

School-Based Prevention

The public school is the one place where tobacco marketing has little chance to swamp the message that tobacco is highly addictive and dangerous. School-based tobacco prevention programs can be effective, according to various government and private studies. The typical effect of a well-designed program seems to be about a 20 percent reduction in tobacco use. The key, however, is to craft a multilayered message that works. Experts say that it is important to focus on the immediate effects of tobacco, not just on the long-term hazards. At least as important is to focus on social norms. As children enter their teenage years, they are strongly influenced by peer behavior. Knowing that about three-quarters of young people do not smoke helps prevent others from taking up the habit, experts say. Providing youth with specific training to resist both marketing and peer pressure is also important, they say. Finally, involving parents and having a credible and appealing spokesperson for the message are key to its effectiveness.

One example of a highly effective antitobacco spokesperson is Patrick Reynolds. As the grandson of R.J. Reynolds, founder of the R.J. Reynolds Tobacco Company, Patrick Reynolds occupies a unique place in the field. After watching his father, elder brother, and other relatives die from the product they were selling, in 1986 he became the first tobacco-industry figure to publicly denounce the cigarette business. In 1989 Reynolds created the Foundation for a Smokefree America. He now spends much of his time addressing school assemblies. There he delivers a powerful message about how his father, a successful tobacco executive, fell ill with cigarette-induced emphysema and died when Patrick was just 15. He goes on to excoriate the marketing of tobacco to youth and to empower young people to resist the temptation to use it. After his visit to Wausau East High School in Wausau, Wisconsin, Principal Bradley J. Peck remarked, "For one solid hour, you could have heard a pin drop in our auditorium."[30]

A Lack of Consistency

Most prevention programs are organized at the individual school level, and thus quality varies widely. Oregon is one state whose school-based tobacco prevention efforts have been singled out for excellence. During the 1999 to 2000 school year, certain schools there adopted a CDC-recommended tobacco prevention approach with multilayered strategies that included teaching near- and long-term health consequences, social consequences (such as clinging offensive odors, stained teeth, and stigma), and peer norms. A study of those schools found that smoking among eighth graders dropped by 22 percent in one year, compared with only an 8 percent decline in schools that did not offer the CDC-endorsed program. Oregon's voters funded the program through a ballot initiative that raised the state's tax on cigarettes by 30 cents a pack.

Unfortunately, research suggests that most school-based programs are substandard. A 2002 study by the American Legacy Foundation finds that only 38 percent of middle-school students and 17 percent of high-school students receive at least 3 of the 4 recommended prevention strategies. Cheryl Healton, president and CEO of the foundation, cites "a distressing gap between what has been demonstrated to be effective and what is practiced in schools."[31]

In any event, not all schools have tobacco-prevention programs, and some do not offer the programs until too late. According to the CDC, 90 percent of high schools offer some tobacco prevention, but only 86 percent of junior high and even fewer elementary schools do the same. Critics point out that smoking starts as early as fifth grade in many cases, and the younger the child, the swifter and deeper the addiction. Another step in reducing tobacco use, therefore, would be to make high-quality tobacco prevention education universal in public schools, starting in the early grades.

> " Research suggests that most school-based [antismoking] programs are substandard. "

Cessation Programs

For the millions who are already tobacco users, the challenges of quitting are steep. In recent years, however, it has become somewhat easier for a motivated addict to kick the habit. There are 2 major reasons for this. First, programs to help smokers or other tobacco users quit have become more sophisticated. Gone are the days of "cold turkey"—attempting to quit all at once—which frequently resulted in disheartening failure. Historically, more than 4 in 5 smokers surveyed have said they want to quit. According to the American Heart Association, up to 40 percent of participants in modern cessation programs succeed in breaking their addiction for good. That is about twice the success rate of traditional tobacco-quitting programs.

The other big advance in cessation is nicotine-replacement therapy. Transdermal patches deliver nicotine through the skin for those attempting to quit smoking. Similarly, nicotine gum gives the addict a dose of nicotine to help him or her get through the process of breaking habits associated with tobacco use. The American Heart Association says that nicotine-replacement therapy doubles the chances of a successful break with tobacco. In the future, additional medical aids to quitting are likely to emerge. Researchers funded by the National Institute on Drug Abuse have found a compound called methoxsalen that significantly reduces a smoker's urge for nicotine. Other breakthroughs may follow as research efforts continue.

Fewer Places to Smoke

Efforts to protect the nonsmoking public from secondhand smoke have had the unintended consequence of inducing some smokers to quit. Studies show that a complete smoking ban in the workplace reduces the proportion of smoking employees by about 4 percent.

When combined with efforts to encourage smokers to quit, the results can be far more dramatic. In New York City, for example, smoking prevalence among adults fell by 11 percent in the year following implementation of a comprehensive smoking ban, a cigarette excise tax increase, a media campaign, and a cessation initiative involving the distribution of free nicotine-replacement therapy kits. Thus, in 2002 some 140,000 New Yorkers kicked the habit.

> **Studies show that a complete smoking ban in the workplace reduces the proportion of smoking employees by about 4 percent.**

Across the nation communities are restricting the number of indoor places where people can smoke. Even some outdoor facilities have become nonsmoking venues. Many sports stadiums, for example, no longer allow smoking. Whole university campuses have gone tobacco-free. In August 2006 Indiana University-Purdue University, Indianapolis, became one of the first large urban universities to ban the use or sale of all tobacco products.

Finally, many states have responded to public pressure to reduce smoking by raising taxes on cigarettes. This has proven an effective deterrent to youth. According to the Campaign for Tobacco-Free Kids, every 10 percent increase in the price of cigarettes reduces youth smoking by about 7 percent. Since 2002 42 of the 50 states have raised cigarette taxes, often quite steeply. In the 4 years from 2002, average per-pack taxes more than doubled to 96 cents; however, the tobacco industry has countered with a new line of discount cigarettes, which some experts say has contributed to a faltering decline of youth smoking prevalence. In addition to all the steps noted above, then, price and accessibility may be significant factors in reducing future tobacco use.

Primary Source Quotes*

How Can Nicotine and Tobacco Use Be Reduced?

66 Just as we cannot separate the war against narcotics and the war against organized crime, so too we cannot separate the war against tobacco from the war against those who have fueled the pandemic tobacco-related illness and death, tobacco transnationals, led by US-based Philip Morris. 99

—Alfred Munzer, quoted in Centers for Disease Control and Prevention, "Public Meeting for Framework Convention on Tobacco Control," March 15, 2000. www.cdc.gov.

Munzer is director of pulmonary medicine at Washington Adventist Hospital and past president of the American Lung Association.

66 Smokers have already been driven away from many workplaces into the street for a furtive puff. But further legal harassment, to the point of what an industry spokesman calls 'backdoor prohibition,' seems unstoppable. Lost in this lynching frenzy: the fact that smoking might be, in some small ways, good for you. 99

—Peter Brimelow, "Thank You for Smoking," July 4, 1994. www.lewrockwell.com.

Brimelow, a former senior editor of *Forbes* magazine, is a libertarian advocate who opposes controls on adult smoking choices.

* Editor's Note: While the definition of a primary source can be narrowly or broadly defined, for the purposes of Compact Research, a primary source consists of: 1) results of original research presented by an organization or researcher; 2) eyewitness accounts of events, personal experience, or work experience; 3) first-person editorials offering pundits' opinions; 4) government officials presenting political plans and/or policies; 5) representatives of organizations presenting testimony or policy.

66 The reduction of illness, disability and death related to smoking is a key public health objective for the United States. We are keenly aware that smoking presents a real threat to public health. The imperative to act at home and abroad is clear. 99

—Tommy G. Thompson, "Remarks of the United States Health and Human Services Secretary Tommy G. Thompson on the Framework Convention on Tobacco Control World Health Assembly," United States Mission—Geneva, May 21, 2003. www.us-mission.ch.

Thompson, then secretary of the U.S. Department of Health and Human Services, made the above remarks at the May 21, 2003, U.S. announcement of support for the Framework Convention on Tobacco Control, a treaty sponsored by the World Health Organization.

66 President Bush committed [the United States] to preventing tobacco use and protecting public health, but he has gone back on his word. The pocket veto of this treaty is yet another wet kiss to Big Tobacco, and it is a disgrace that this country will not be able to participate in global negotiations because of the president's inaction. 99

—Tom Harkin, "Bush Pocket Veto of Global Treaty Another Wet Kiss to Big Tobacco," November 7, 2005. http://harkin.senate.gov.

Harkin, a Democrat, represents Iowa in the U.S. Senate.

66 Meat consumption is just as dangerous to public health as tobacco use. 99

—Neal Barnard, news release, September 23, 1999. www.activistcash.com.

Barnard is a physician, president of the Physicians Committee for Responsible Medicine, and a medical adviser to the animal rights group People for the Ethical Treatment of Animals.

66 The . . . decline in cancer death rates among men is due in large part to their substantial decrease in tobacco use. We need to enhance efforts to reduce tobacco use in women so that the rate of decline in cancer death rates becomes comparable to that of men. 99

Betsy A. Kohler, quoted in National Cancer Institute, "Annual Report to the Nation Finds Cancer Death Rates Continue to Drop; Lower Cancer Rates Observed in U.S. Latino Populations," September 6, 2006. www.cancer.gov.

Kohler is president of the North American Association of Central Cancer Registries, a professional organization that develops and promotes uniform data standards for tracking and reducing the incidence of cancer.

66 Truth was an early victim in the battle against tobacco. The big lie, repeated ad nauseam in anti-tobacco circles, is that smoking causes more than 400,000 premature deaths each year in the United States. That mantra is the principal justification for all manner of tobacco regulations and legislation, not to mention lawsuits by dozens of states. 99

—Robert A. Levy and Rosalind B. Marimont, "Lies, Damned Lies, & 400,000 Smoking-Related Deaths," *Regulation*, vol. 21, no. 4, 1998. www.cato.org.

Levy is a senior fellow in constitutional studies at the Cato Institute and an adjunct professor at Georgetown University Law Center. Marimont, a mathematician and scientist, retired after a career with the National Institute of Standards and Technology (formerly the Bureau of Standards).

66 Levy and Marimont's arguments do not present a scientifically sound and convincing case that the estimate of 400,000 annual smoking-related deaths is a specious, statistical gimmick. 99

—Elizabeth M. Whelan and Alicia M. Lukachko, "A Critical Assessment of 'Lies, Damned Lies, & 400,000 Smoking-Related Deaths' by Robert Levy and Rosalind Marimont, published in *Regulation*, Fall 1998," American Council on Science and Health, October 1, 1999. www.acsh.org.

Whelan, president and founder of the American Council on Science and Health, holds a doctorate in public health from Harvard University. Lukachko, who holds a master's degree in public health, is the council's assistant director of public health.

66 Reading the FDCA [Food, Drug, and Cosmetic Act] as a whole, as well as in conjunction with Congress' subsequent tobacco-specific legislation, it is plain that Congress has not given the FDA the authority to regulate tobacco products as customarily marketed. 99

—Sandra Day O'Connor, *FDA v. Brown & Williamson Tobacco Corp.* (98-1152). www.law.cornell.edu.

U.S. Supreme Court Justice O'Connor, the first woman to serve on the nation's highest judicial body, wrote the majority opinion in the above-cited case. She retired in 2005.

66 Whenever anybody challenges the view that 'tobacco kills,' they are immediately confronted with the argument that they are tools of the giant tobacco companies. 99

—Lauren A. Colby, *In Defense of Smokers*, self-published, 2004. www.lcolby.com.

Colby is the author of a book titled *In Defense of Smokers*, which he claims debunks most of the scientific studies that underlie official pronouncements about the dangers of smoking.

66 Cigarette tax increases and comprehensive tobacco prevention programs are the equivalent of a vaccine that can inoculate our kids against tobacco use and the addiction, disease and death that result. Governors and legislators across the country should act now to provide this vaccine to every child. 99

—Matthew L. Myers, quoted in Campaign for Tobacco-Free Kids, "Landmark National Cancer Institute Report Concludes Cigarette Tax Increases and Tobacco Prevention Programs Reduce Youth Smoking," April 2, 2002. www.tobaccofreekids.org.

Myers, an attorney and former Federal Trade Commission staff member, is president of the Campaign for Tobacco-Free Kids.

❝We are encouraged by the continued decline in cigarette smoking among U.S. adults and want to congratulate those who have successfully quit. Quitting smoking is the most important step smokers can take to improve their overall health and reduce their risk of disease.❞

—Julie Gerberding, quoted in Centers for Disease Control and Prevention, "Lower Adult Smoking Rates with More Adults Quitting," November 10, 2005. www.cdc.gov.

Gerberding was appointed director of the U.S. Centers for Disease Control and Prevention in 2002. She also serves as an associate professor of medicine at Emory University in Atlanta.

❝A smokefree U.S. is achievable. Going smokefree will result in healthier people, reduced health care costs and thousands of lives saved.❞

—John L. Kirkwood, quoted in American Lung Association, "American Lung Association Challenges States to Go Smokefree by 2010," American Lung Association, January 10, 2006. www.lungusa.org.

Kirkwood is president and chief executive officer of the American Lung Association, which advocates tobacco control and healthy air quality.

Facts and Illustrations

How Can Nicotine and Tobacco Use Be Reduced?

- Nearly 1 billion men and about a quarter of a billion women around the world smoke.

- In 2000 an estimated 5.5 trillion cigarettes were smoked. That is about 15 billion a day, in a world of just over 6 billion people.

- Female smoking is most prevalent in developed countries of the West, where about 22 percent of women smoke.

- In the United States, smoking rates have been falling since 1976.

- According to the U.S. Centers for Disease Control and Prevention, the health costs associated with smoking amount to more than $10 per cigarette pack sold.

- Some 42 states and several U.S. territories have raised taxes on cigarettes since 2002. Of those, 20 states raised the taxes by at least a dollar.

- Every state that has raised cigarette taxes has seen revenues go up and smoking go down, according to the Campaign for Tobacco-Free Kids.

- Experts say that higher prices and new tobacco taxes have helped cut tobacco use among eighth graders by more than 50 percent since the mid-1990s.

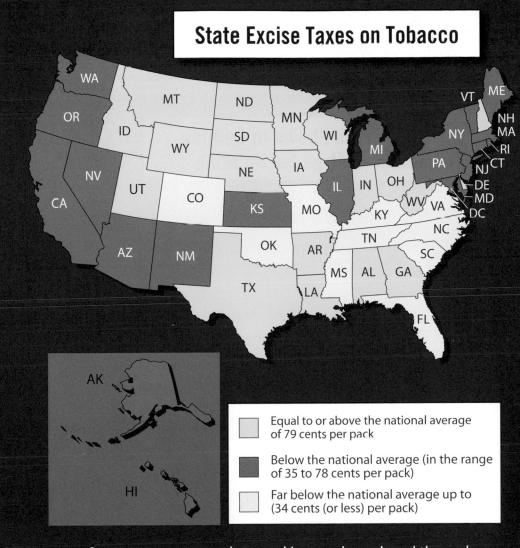

State Excise Taxes on Tobacco

Legend:
- Equal to or above the national average of 79 cents per pack
- Below the national average (in the range of 35 to 78 cents per pack)
- Far below the national average up to (34 cents (or less) per pack)

Some experts argue that smoking can be reduced through increased taxes. This map shows how taxes on tobacco vary by state. The western, midwestern, and northeastern states have the highest tobacco tax while the southeast states have the lowest.

Source: American Cancer Society, 2004.

- Marketing to youth continues. New flavored cigarettes with youth-oriented names like "Twista Lime" appeal to more than twice as many teens as they do to smokers over age 19.

- Kentucky is the state with the highest rate of smoking—nearly 29 percent—and the highest rate of cancer deaths—228 per 100,000 residents.

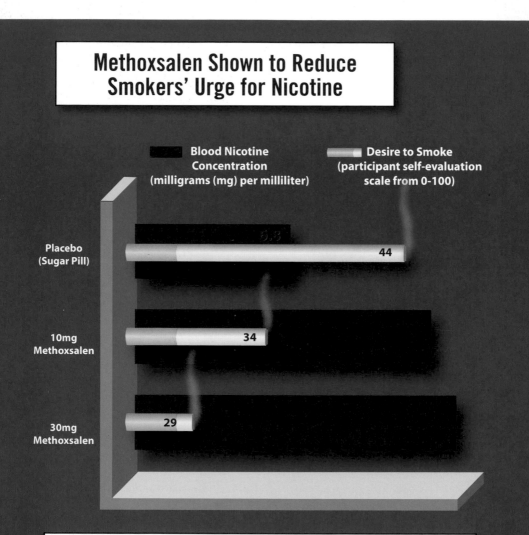

Methoxsalen Shown to Reduce Smokers' Urge for Nicotine

Blood Nicotine Concentration (milligrams (mg) per milliliter)

Desire to Smoke (participant self-evaluation scale from 0-100)

Placebo (Sugar Pill): 0.8, 44

10mg Methoxsalen: 34

30mg Methoxsalen: 29

Experimental evidence shows that a medication called Methoxsalen can help smokers quit by boosting and prolonging the effect of nicotine on the body. The study shows that the more Methoxsalen taken, the higher the blood nicotine concentration and the lower the desire to smoke.

Source: National Institute on Drug Abuse. www.nida.nih.gov.

Medicaid Coverage of Smoking Cessation Treatments

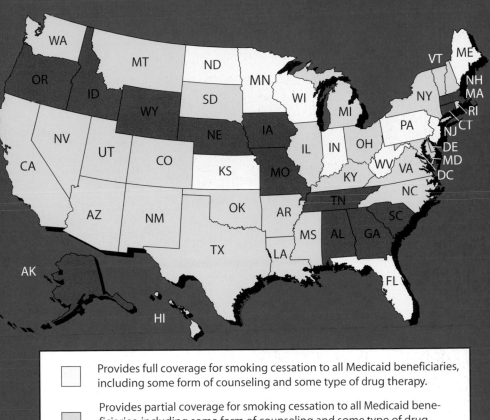

Provides full coverage for smoking cessation to all Medicaid beneficiaries, including some form of counseling and some type of drug therapy.

Provides partial coverage for smoking cessation to all Medicaid beneficiaries, including some form of counseling and some type of drug therapy.

No state requirements to cover Medicaid beneficiaries for smoking cessation treatments.

This map shows state Medicaid (a government health insurance program for low-income individuals and families) coverage for smoking cessation treatments. Some experts argue that insurance coverage of cessation programs should increase to help reduce smoking.

Source: Centers for Disease Control and Prevention, 2004. www.cdc.gov.

Projected Changes in Cigarette Consumption Worldwide, 1998–2008

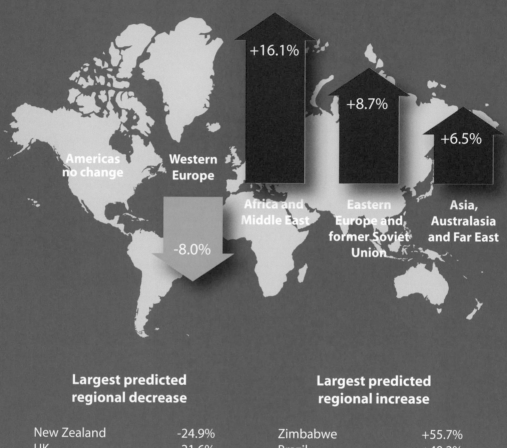

+16.1%

+8.7%

+6.5%

Americas
no change

Western
Europe

Africa and
Middle East

Eastern
Europe and
former Soviet
Union

Asia,
Australasia
and Far East

-8.0%

Largest predicted regional decrease		Largest predicted regional increase	
New Zealand	-24.9%	Zimbabwe	+55.7%
UK	-21.6%	Brazil	+40.2%
South Africa	-17.3%	Pakistan	+35.9%
US	-13.0%	Norway	+30.5%
Czech Republic	-2.5%	Latvia	+26.5%

This illustration shows that from 1998 to 2008, smoking is projected to increase by more than 16 percent in Africa and the Middle East; however, the smoking level in the Americas is expected to remain constant, while smoking in western Europe will drop by 8 percent.

Source: *The Christian Science Monitor*, 2005.

- Between 1998, when the tobacco companies agreed to fund anti-smoking efforts, by 2005, cigarette smoking in the United States dropped 20 percent.

- Some 140 countries have ratified an international treaty to curtail tobacco use. The United States initially signed the treaty but has not ratified it.

Key People and Advocacy Groups

James Buchanan Duke: Duke built his family's North Carolina tobacco business into the dominant tobacco company in America by the beginning of the twentieth century. Following a 1906 antitrust trial, his American Tobacco Company was broken up into several companies, which went on to become leading U.S. tobacco companies in their own right.

Stanton Glantz: A medical professor, Glantz has been nicknamed the Ralph Nader of antitobacco activists. His reputation apparently motivated a disaffected tobacco-industry insider to send him thousands of incriminating documents in 1994. The find helped show that the industry had been covering up the dangers of its products.

David R. Hardy: Hardy earned a reputation as the top defense attorney for the tobacco industry. His Kansas City firm, Shook, Hardy & Bacon, successfully defended tobacco companies against dozens of lawsuits by employing a strategy Hardy outlined in 1970: to keep close wraps on all industry doubts about the safety of their product.

David Kessler: While serving as commissioner of the Food and Drug Administration during the Clinton administration, Kessler led a fight to have nicotine regulated as a drug. Congress and the courts eventually rejected that policy, but Kessler, who became dean of Yale University's medical school, continued to speak out for restrictions on tobacco sales.

Bennett S. LeBow: As chief executive officer of the company that owned Liggett Tobacco, Bennett S. LeBow stunned the industry when he broke ranks with the other tobacco companies in 1996 to announce that he would settle a lawsuit brought by state attorneys general. Although Liggett was the smallest of the defendants, the others all followed suit.

Yumiko Mochizuki: Mochizuki was appointed director of the World Health Organization's Tobacco Free Initiative in September 2005. In that position, she leads the UN-related body's effort to actualize international commitments to reduce global tobacco use. Mochizuki previously headed up the Japanese Ministry of Health's development of tobacco-control policies and took part in the preparation of the World Health Organization's Framework Convention on Tobacco Control.

Mike Moore: As attorney general for Mississippi, Moore filed a lawsuit against tobacco companies that ended in the landmark Master Settlement Agreement of 1998. Tobacco companies admitted for the first time that their product was dangerous and addictive and agreed to curtail advertising and to fund smoking-prevention campaigns aimed at youth.

Philip Morris: The 19th-century tobacconist began a cigarette business in London in 1854. It would eventually grow into the world's largest tobacco company, bearing his name.

Matthew L. Myers: Myers, an attorney who began his involvement with tobacco as a staff member for the Federal Trade Commission—responsible for regulating tobacco advertising—went on to lead a coalition of antismoking organizations. In that role he helped shape legislation and court cases restricting tobacco. He is now president of the Campaign for Tobacco-Free Kids.

Jean Nicot: Sent by France on a diplomatic mission to Portugal, Nicot became fascinated by tobacco there. After experimenting with it, he took some back to France in 1600, where he convinced the queen that it had great medicinal properties. Nicotine is named for him.

Jeffrey Wigand: Wigand served as vice president for research and development for Brown & Williamson Tobacco Corporation from December 1988 to March 1993. After leaving his employment with Brown & Williamson, he cooperated with government agencies investigating the tobacco industry and in 1995 gained fame as a whistle-blower on the tobacco industry when he gave an interview to CBS's *60 Minutes*.

Chronology

1492
Native Americans give Columbus tobacco leaves as a gift; he throws them away.

1791
London physician John Hill reports cases in which snuff appears to have caused nasal cancers.

1950
The first major epidemiological study to definitively link smoking to lung cancer is published in the *Journal of the American Medical Association*.

1665
The poisonous nature of tobacco is revealed when a cat dies shortly after being fed a drop of oil distilled from tobacco leaves.

1847
Philip Morris, whose name is now associated with the world's largest tobacco company, opens a London shop to sell hand-rolled cigarettes.

| 1500 | 1600 | 1700 | 1800 | 1900 | 1940 | 1950 | 1950 | 1960 |

1560
French naturalist Jean Nicot experiments with tobacco as a medicine and then writes to the queen of France on its supposed curative properties.

1809
French chemist Louis Nicolas Vanquelin isolates nicotine from tobacco.

1953
Researcher Ernst Wynder publishes a landmark study showing that painting cigarette tar on the backs of mice creates tumors.

1963
U.S. per-capita adult smoking rates peak at 4,336 annually, or about 12 cigarettes per day. About half of all American men and a third of American women smoke.

1753
Swedish botanist Carolus Linnaeus classifies tobacco in the plant genus *nicotiana*, after Jean Nicot.

1913
The R.J. Reynolds company introduces Camel brand cigarettes.

The organization now known as the American Cancer Society is formed.

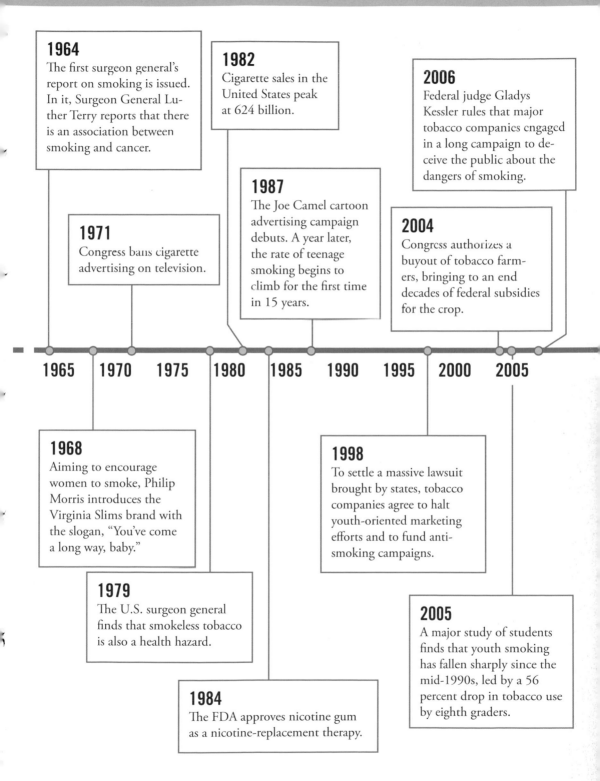

1964
The first surgeon general's report on smoking is issued. In it, Surgeon General Luther Terry reports that there is an association between smoking and cancer.

1982
Cigarette sales in the United States peak at 624 billion.

2006
Federal judge Gladys Kessler rules that major tobacco companies engaged in a long campaign to deceive the public about the dangers of smoking.

1987
The Joe Camel cartoon advertising campaign debuts. A year later, the rate of teenage smoking begins to climb for the first time in 15 years.

1971
Congress bans cigarette advertising on television.

2004
Congress authorizes a buyout of tobacco farmers, bringing to an end decades of federal subsidies for the crop.

1965   1970   1975   1980   1985   1990   1995   2000   2005

1968
Aiming to encourage women to smoke, Philip Morris introduces the Virginia Slims brand with the slogan, "You've come a long way, baby."

1998
To settle a massive lawsuit brought by states, tobacco companies agree to halt youth-oriented marketing efforts and to fund anti-smoking campaigns.

1979
The U.S. surgeon general finds that smokeless tobacco is also a health hazard.

2005
A major study of students finds that youth smoking has fallen sharply since the mid-1990s, led by a 56 percent drop in tobacco use by eighth graders.

1984
The FDA approves nicotine gum as a nicotine-replacement therapy.

Related Organizations

Action on Smoking and Health (ASH)

2013 H St. NW

Washington, DC 20006

phone: (202) 659-4310

Web site: www.ash.org

ASH is a nonprofit antismoking organization based in the United States. Its principal activity is to serve as the legal-action arm of the nonsmoking community, bringing or joining in legal actions concerning smoking and ensuring that the voice of the nonsmoker is heard. It also serves as a public advocate of the nonsmokers' rights movement.

Altria Group

120 Park Ave., 16th Floor

New York, NY 10017

phone: (917) 663-4000

Web Site: www.altria.com

Altria is the corporate parent of Philip Morris, the world's largest tobacco company in terms of revenue (The China National Tobacco Company and Japan Tobacco move more product but for less income.) Philip Morris's lineup of cigarettes is led by Marlboro, the most popular worldwide brand. Philip Morris was started in 1847 by a London tobacconist of the same name.

American Cancer Society (ACS)

1599 Clifton Rd. NE

Atlanta, GA 30329

phone: (800) 227-2345

Web site: www.cancer.org

The ACS is a nationwide voluntary health organization dedicated to eliminating cancer as a major health problem through research, education, advocacy, and service. The ACS has been a leader in the effort to promote smoking cessation and in legal and public policy efforts to restrict tobacco advertising. It was founded in 1913 by a group of doctors in New York City.

American Heart Association

7272 Greenville Ave.

Dallas, TX 75231

phone: (214) 706-1925

Web site: www.americanheart.org

The American Heart Association, which traces its origins back to 1913, works to combat cardiovascular disease and its effects. In recent years the association has taken increasing by strong stands on the dangers of tobacco use to public health. Its commitment to tobacco control includes promoting smoke-free air policies, excise taxes on tobacco, and funding for tobacco-prevention and treatment programs.

American Legacy Foundation

2030 M St. NW, 6th Floor

Washington, DC 20036

phone: (202) 454-5555

Web site: www.americanlegacy.org

The American Legacy Foundation was created in March 1999 as a result of the Master Settlement Agreement between state attorneys general and the tobacco industry to counter a sharp rise in tobacco use by American youth. Funded primarily by tobacco industry payments from the settlement, the foundation has created a variety of antitobacco public education campaigns, most notably the youth-designed and youth-directed Truth campaign. Its industry funding has mostly expired, but it continues to seek funding to carry on its mission of deterring young people from taking up tobacco and helping those who do gain access to cessation programs.

American Lung Association

61 Broadway, 6th Floor

New York, NY 10006

phone: (800) 586-4872

Web site: www.lungusa.org

The American Lung Association is the oldest voluntary health organization in the United States. Founded in 1904 to fight tuberculosis, the association was one of the first health organizations to join the fight for tobacco control in the early 1960s. It continues to be a major partner in various lawsuits and lobbying efforts to restrict exposure to tobacco smoke.

Americans for Nonsmokers' Rights (ANR)

2530 San Pablo Ave., Suite J

Berkeley, CA 94702

phone: (510) 841-3032

Web site: www.no-smoke.org

ANR is a national organization that lobbies for nonsmokers' rights. Formerly known as the Group Against Smoking Pollution, it confronts the tobacco industry at all levels of government, seeking to protect nonsmokers from exposure to secondhand smoke and to prevent tobacco addiction among youth. ANR was formed in 1976 and remains a member-supported organization.

Campaign for Tobacco-Free Kids

1400 Eye St., Suite 1200

Washington, DC 20005

phone: (202) 296-5469

Web site: www.tobaccofreekids.org

The Campaign for Tobacco-Free Kids is a not-for-profit advocacy organization whose aim is to prevent young people from becoming addicted to nicotine and being exposed to secondhand smoke. It was founded in 1995. Since then it has participated in multiple lawsuits against the tobacco industry and has lobbied at all levels of government.

Council for Tobacco Research–USA

122 E. 42nd St., Room 2518

New York , NY 10168

Web site: www.ctr-usa.org

The Council for Tobacco Research–USA was created by a consortium of tobacco companies with a mandate to research tobacco and health issues. Critics charge that its true mission is to cast doubt on the link between smoking and lung cancer. Following the 1998 Master Settlement Agreement the council became an online repository for various documents related to smoking and health.

FORCES International

PO Box 533

Sutton, WV 26601

phone: (304) 765-5394

Web site: www.forces.org

FORCES International is a nonprofit organization representing the interests of smokers. The acronym stands for Fight Ordinances and Restrictions to Control and Eliminate Smoking. It was founded in 1995 to fight what it claims is junk science regarding the hazards of secondhand smoke. Standing on libertarian principles, it also opposes school-based tobacco-prevention programs, which it regards as state indoctrination of youth.

Foundation for a Smokefree America

PO Box 492028

Los Angeles, CA 90049-8028

phone: (310) 471-4270

Web site: www.anti-smoking.org

The Foundation for a Smokefree America was founded in 1989 by Patrick Reynolds, a grandson of the founder of the R.J. Reynolds Tobacco Company, after tobacco use killed some of his closest relatives. He quit smoking, sold his R.J. Reynolds stock, and became an influential advocate for a smoke-free America. The foundation supports his efforts to prevent youth from trying tobacco and to promote a tobacco-free future.

R.J. Reynolds Tobacco Company

PO Box 2990

Winston-Salem, NC 27102-2990

phone: (336) 741-7693

Web site: www.reynoldsamerican.com

R.J. Reynolds is the world's second-largest tobacco company in terms of revenues. It was founded by Richard Joshua Reynolds in 1874 and grew to become an international purveyor of many of the world's leading cigarette brands, including Camel, Winston, and Kool. In 2003 it entered an agreement to absorb Brown & Williamson, another major American tobacco firm. The conglomerate is now known as ReynoldsAmerican. (Note: the company has a policy of only responding to inquiries from adults, and only if sent through its Web site.)

Smoker's Club Inc.

PO Box 814

Center Conway, NH 03813

The Smoker's Club is an all-volunteer nonprofit organization providing information and arguments to smokers seeking to oppose bans on smoking. It also provides members with monthly newsletters and access to online forums for smokers to socialize and exchange information.

Smokers Fighting Discrimination

PO Box 5472

Katy, TX 77491

e-mail: SFD-USA-owner@yahoogroups.com

Smokers Fighting Discrimination is organized as a 501(c)(4) nonprofit, meaning it can lobby elected officials, support legislation on behalf of the interests of smokers, and rally grassroots support for nonpartisan issues. It can also share endorsements of federal candidates for office with the organization's membership. Contributions to the organization are not tax deductible. The group was founded in 1996.

Tobacco Institute

Web site: www.tobaccoinstitute.com

The Tobacco Institute was created as the umbrella trade-advocacy organization for the U.S. tobacco industry. It lobbied and funded research friendly to the tobacco industry. Following the 1998 settlement of the state attorneys general lawsuit, it has limited its Internet presence to providing documents related to smoking and health.

U.S. Centers for Disease Control and Prevention (CDC), Office on Smoking and Health

1600 Clifton Rd.

Atlanta, GA 30333

phone: (404) 639-3534

Web site: www.cdc.gov

The Office on Smoking and Health is a division within the National Center for Chronic Disease Prevention and Health Promotion, which is one of the centers within the CDC. The CDC is the federal government's chief body of agencies devoted to preventing the spread of disease.

World Health Organization (WHO)

Avenue Appia 20

1211 Geneva 27

Switzerland

Web site: www.who.int

WHO is a UN body whose special mission is to promote health. Established in 1948, WHO's objective, as set forth in its constitution, is the attainment of the highest possible level of health by all peoples. Tobacco control has become a high priority for WHO, as embodied in the Framework Convention on Tobacco Control, an international treaty that WHO proposed and is now overseeing.

For Further Research

Books

Richard Craze, *Stop Smoking, Stay Cool: A Dedicated Smoker's Guide to Not Smoking.* Devon, UK: White Ladder, 2006.

Federal Trade Commission, *Up in Smoke: The Truth About Tar and Nicotine Ratings.* Washington, DC: Federal Trade Commission, Bureau of Consumer Protection, Office of Consumer and Business Education, 2000.

Roberta Ferrence et al., eds., *Nicotine and Public Health.* Washington, DC: American Public Health Association, 2000.

Hanan Frenk and Reuven Dar, *A Critique of Nicotine Addiction.* Boston: Kluwer Academic, 2000.

Prabhat Jha and Frank J. Chaloupka, eds., *Tobacco Control in Developing Countries.* New York: Oxford University Press, 2000.

Kathleen Meister et al., eds., *Cigarettes: What the Warning Label Doesn't Tell You.* 2nd ed. New York: American Council on Science and Health, 2003.

David B. Moyer, *The Tobacco Book.* Santa Fe, NM: Sunstone, 2005.

Don Oakley, *Slow Burn: The Great American Antismoking Scam (and Why It Will Fail).* Gainsesville, VA: Eyrie, 1999.

Fred C. Pampel, *Tobacco Industry and Smoking.* New York : Facts On File, 2004.

Leah Ranney et al., *Tobacco Use: Prevention, Cessation, and Control.* Rockville, MD: Agency for Healthcare Research and Quality, 2006.

Robert G. Robinson et al., *Pathways to Freedom: Winning the Fight Against Tobacco.* Atlanta: Centers for Disease Control and Prevention, 2006.

Diana K. Sergis, Cipollone v. Liggett Group: *Suing Tobacco Companies.* Berkeley Heights, NJ: Enslow, 2001.

U.S. Deptartment of Health and Human Services, Public Health Service, National Institutes of Health, National Cancer Institute, *Risks*

Associated with Smoking Cigarettes with Low Machine-Measured Yields of Tar and Nicotine. Bethesda, MD: National Institutes of Health, 2001.

U.S. Surgeon General, *Health Consequences of Involuntary Exposure to Tobacco Smoke: A Report of the Surgeon General.* Atlanta: Centers for Disease Control and Prevention, 2006.

Periodicals

Center for the Advancement of Health, "Smoke-Filled Cars: New Fodder for the Next Clean Air Fight," *ScienceDaily,* October 4, 2006. www.sciencedaily.com.

Charleston (WV) Daily Mail, editorial, "Over-Regulation Is a Bad Habit, Too: Consenting Adults Have the Right to Associate Freely in Smoky Bars," October 4, 2006. www.dailymail.com.

Krisha McCoy, "Smokers May Be More Likely to Contract HIV," *Health-Day,* September 21, 2006. www.healthday.com.

Robert Preidt, "Genes May Tie Smoking, Drinking," *HealthDay,* April 24, 2006. www.healthday.com.

William Reid, "Tobacco Settlement Monies Went Up in Smoke for Blacks," *Black World Today,* June 26, 2002. www.tbwt.org.

Marisa Schultz, Amy Lee, and Eric Lacy, "Workers Fume as Firms Ban Smoking at Home," *Detroit News,* January 27, 2005.

Michael Siegel, "On the Deafening Silence of the Tobacco Control Movement: The Need for Some Moral Courage," *Rest of the Story: Tobacco News Analysis and Commentary,* October 5, 2006. http://tobaccoanalysis.blogspot.com.

P.D. Thacker, "Pundit for Hire: Smoked Out," *New Republic,* February 2, 2006.

Michael J. Thun, editorial, "More Misleading Science from the Tobacco Industry," *British Medical Journal,* July 30, 2003.

Elizabeth M. Whelan, "The Intolerance and Arrogance of the Modern-Day Anti-Smoking Movement," *American Council on Science and Health,* April 21, 2006.

V.M. White et al., "Cigarette Promotional Offers: Who Takes Advantage?" *American Journal of Preventive Medicine*, March 2006.

Thomas Zeltner et al., "Tobacco Company Strategies to Undermine Tobacco Control Activities at the World Health Organization," *World Health Organization Report, 2000*. www.who.int.

Web Sites

Anti-Smoking.org (www.anti-smoking.org) This youth-oriented Web site is operated by the Foundation for a Smokefree America. It includes tips on quitting, resources for research on tobacco, and tips on how to speak out against tobacco use.

FOREST (www.forestonline.org) This London-based group (the acronym stands for Freedom Organisation for the Right to Enjoy Smoking Tobacco) offers news and opinion on subjects related to smokers' rights. It includes an online magazine and also offers advice for smokers on subjects such as air-cleaning devices.

Philip Morris Tobacco Documents (www.pmdocs.com) This Web site is maintained by the Philip Morris USA tobacco company to provide the public with access to documents produced during lawsuits by state attorneys general. The documents will span the period from October 23, 1998, through June 30, 2010.

Smoking and Minorities (academic.udayton.edu) This site, based at the University of Dayton in Ohio, contains a wealth of information about the marketing of cigarettes to minorities, especially African Americans. It includes documents from the tobacco industry that were released in the course of litigation.

Smokinglobby.com (www.smokinglobby.com) Smokinglobby.com is an online forum for discussion of smokers' rights. The organization opposes heavy taxation of tobacco and most restrictions concerning where and when people can smoke. It claims that smoking is not nearly as harmful as popular opinion claims.

The Smoking Section (www.smokingsection.com) The home of "Smokers with Attitude," this site contains numerous essays inveighing against antitobacco statutes. It also hosts a bookstore and forum for smokers.

The Truth Campaign (www.thetruth.com) This is the site of the American Legacy Foundation's hard-edged antismoking campaign. It includes excerpts from its reality television ads, photos from the campaign's tour, and even ringtones.

Tobacco Documents Online (tobaccodocuments.org) This is a vast repository of documents produced during litigation. Although registration is required, there is no charge for searching the documents. The site is run by the Smokefree Network, which collaborated with the American Legacy Foundation in creating the online repository following the 1998 Master Settlement Agreement.

Tobacco.org (www.tobacco.org) This site, run by the Smokefree Network, contains numerous news stories about tobacco-related issues. It also has an extensive quotations page and links.

Tobacco Control Archives at UCSF (http://galen.library.ucsf.edu) The University of California at San Francisco operates this vast online archive of tobacco-related documents. It includes millions of documents concerning scientific research, manufacturing, marketing, advertising, and sales of cigarettes.

Tobacco Survivors United (www.tobaccosurvivorsunited.org) Tobacco Survivors United is a network of survivors, families, and friends of men and women who have overcome the damaging effects of tobacco products. The site includes a large archive of articles on tobacco-related issues.

Women and Smoking (www.cdc.gov) This site centers on the surgeon general's report on women and smoking. It includes press releases, fact sheets, and the 2001 report itself.

Source Notes

Overview

1. Quoted in Roseanne Skirble, "Sixteen Million New Cancer Cases Expected by 2020 Worldwide," *Voice of America News*, July 20, 2006. www.voanews.com.
2. Mark Twain, "Smoking." www.twain quotes.com.
3. Quoted in Mark H. Anderson, Brian Blackstone, and Christina Cheddar Berk, "Tobacco Loses DOJ Case; Escapes Financial Penalties," Dow Jones Newswires, August 17, 2006. www. tobacco.org.
4. Quoted in Anderson, Blackstone, and Berk, "Tobacco Loses DOJ Case."
5. Quoted in Jonathan Leake, "'Safe Cigarette' Claimed to Cut Cancer by 90%," *Sunday Times* (London), November 6, 2005. www.timesonline.co.uk.
6. Quoted in Global Youth Tobacco Survey Collaborating Group, "Differences in Worldwide Tobacco Use by Gender: Findings from the Global Youth Tobacco Survey," February 22, 2005. www.cdc.gov.
7. Gro Harlem Brundtland, foreword to *The Tobacco Atlas*, by Judith Mackay and Michael Eriksen, World Health Organization, 2002, p. 9.
8. Richard Peto and Alan D. Lopez, "The Future Worldwide Health Effects of Current Smoking Patterns," news release, Clinical Trial Service Unit, Oxford University, August 2, 2000. www.ctsu.ox.ac.uk.
9. Quoted in Duke Medical News, "Medical Uses for Nicotine," August 10, 2001. www.dukemednews.org.
10. Quoted in Belinda Rhodes, "Tobacco Firms Won't Be Stubbed Out," *BBC World Service*, September 27, 2006. http://news.bbc.co.uk.

How Harmful Are Nicotine and Tobacco?

11. Associated Press, "Cigarette Addiction Can Start Early," September 11, 2000. http://scienceu.fsu.edu.

How Dangerous Is Exposure to Secondhand Smoke?

12. William Osteen, "The United States Federal Court Decision," FORCES International. www.forces.org.
13. American Lung Association, "Secondhand Smoke," March 2006. www.lung usa.org.
14. Joe Jackson, "The Smoking Issue," 2004. www.joejackson.com.
15. Michael Crichton, "Aliens Cause Global Warming," January 17, 2003. www.crichton-official.com.
16. James E. Enstrom and Geoffrey C. Kabat, "Environmental Tobacco Smoke and Tobacco Related Mortality in a Prospective Study of Californians, 1960–98," *British Medical Journal.* May 17, 2003, p. 1,057. http://bmj.bmjjournals.com.
17. Martha Perske, "Cherry-picked Science on Secondhand Smoke," Junkscience. com February 19, 2001. www.junksci ence.com.
18. U.S. Department of Health and Human Services, *The Health Consequences of Involuntary Exposure to Tobacco Smoke: A Report of the Surgeon General,* Executive Summary. Washington, DC: U.S. Department of Health and Human Services, 2006, p. iii.
19. U.S. Department of Health and Human Services, *The Health Consequences of Involuntary Exposure to Tobacco Smoke,* p. 9.
20. Richard H. Carmona, "Remarks at Press Conference to Launch *Health*

Consequences of Involuntary Exposure to Tobacco Smoke: A Report of the Surgeon General," June 27, 2006. www.surgeongeneral.gov.

Why Do Many Young People Smoke or Chew Tobacco?

21. American Heart Association, "Tobacco Industry's Targeting of Youth, Minorities and Women," 2006. www.americanheart.org.
22. University of Michigan News Service, "Decline in Teen Smoking Appears to Be Nearing Its End," December 19, 2005. www.monitoringthefuture.org.
23. University of Michigan News Service, "Decline in Teen Smoking Appears to Be Nearing Its End".
24. Jim Lobe, "Tobacco Companies Pressed to Halt Youth Smoking Prevention Campaigns," OneWorld U.S., October 25, 2005. www.tobacco.org.

How Can Nicotine and Tobacco Use Be Reduced?

25. Michael Siegel, letter to the Federal Trade Commission, May 17, 2001. www.ftc.gov.
26. Office on Smoking and Health, CDC, "Cigarette Use Among High School Students United States, 1991–2005," *Morbidity and Mortality Weekly Report,* July 7, 2006. www.cdc.gov.
27. Quoted in "Smoking in Movies Gets Kids Hooked," KRON, November 13, 2003. www.kron4.com.
28. Thomas N. Robinson and J.D. Killen, "Do Cigarette Warning Labels Reduce Smoking? Paradoxical Effects Among Adolescents," *Archives of Pediatrics & Adolescent Medicine,* vol. 151, March 1997. www.archpedi.ama.assn.org.
29. Joel M. Moskowitz, "Impact of the 'Truth' Campaign on Cigarette Smoking," *American Journal of Public Health,* March 31, 2005. www.ajph.org.
30. Quoted in "What Past Clients Say," Tobaccofree.org. www.tobaccofree.org.
31. Quoted in Mary Herdoiza, "Study Finds that Multi-Strategy, School-Based Tobacco Prevention Programs Can Reduce Youth Smoking," American Legacy Foundation news release, March 13, 2002. www.americanlegacy.org.

List of Illustrations

How Harmful Are Nicotine and Tobacco?

How Dangerous Is Exposure to Secondhand Smoke?

Why Do Many Young People Smoke or Chew Tobacco?

How Can Nicotine and Tobacco Use Be Reduced?

Index

About the Author

Clay Farris Naff is a journalist, writer, and nonprofit executive. He served as a UPI correspondent in Tokyo in the 1980s and 1990s and later wrote a book about social change in Japan, which won a fellowship award from the National Endowment for the Humanities. Since returning to the United States, he has written widely on science and religion and has edited numerous books on scientific topics. Naff serves as executive director of the Lincoln Literacy Council in Lincoln, Nebraska.